CRUSHING IT WITH FACEBOOK ADS:

The Beginner's Guide to lowering acquisition costs and expanding your customer base with Facebook Advertising in 2019

Table of Contents

Introduction

Chapter 1: Creating Your First Ad

Chapter 2: The First Path to Success – Hit it with Many Ads

Chapter 3: Analyzing Advertising Performance

Chapter 4: Data Breakdowns

Chapter 5: Audience Insights

Chapter 6: Creating Lookalike Audiences

Chapter 7: Creative Types

Chapter 8: ROI - Facebook Goals and Marketing Strategies

Chapter 9: Boosted and Promoted Posts

Chapter 10: Facebook Pixel

Chapter 11: Common Mistakes

© Copyright 2019 Tapless Games. All rights reserved.

The information contained in this manuscript is believed to be accurate and reliable. However, neither the author or publisher guarantee the accuracy of the content contained herein. The author and publisher are not responsible for any errors or ommissions contained herein and are not responsible for any actions, losses, or damages that arise from using this information. This book is provided with the understanding that the author and publisher are supplying information only, and are not responsible for any results from actions taken by readers using this information. The author and publisher are not providing engineering or consulting or professional services of any kind. The author and publisher are not in any way responsible for use of Facebook Advertising services by any reader or any financial losses that may result. If professional services are required, the assistance of such services should be sought by the reader.

Purchasing this book is consent to the fact that both the publisher and the author of this book are in no way rendering service as experts on the topics discussed within and that any recommendations or suggestions that are made herein are for entertainment purposes only. Professionals should be consulted as needed prior to undertaking any of the action endorsed herein.

Furthermore, the transmission, duplication or reproduction of any of the following work including specific information will be considered an illegal act irrespective of if it is done electronically or in print. This extends to creating a secondary or tertiary copy of the work or a recorded copy and is only allowed with express written consent from the Publisher. All additional right reserved.

The information in the following pages is broadly considered to be a truthful and accurate account of facts and as such any inattention, use or misuse of the information in question by the reader will render any resulting actions solely under their purview. There are no scenarios in which the publisher or the original author of this work can be in any fashion deemed liable for any hardship or damages that may befall them after undertaking information described herein.

Additionally, the information in the following pages is intended only for informational purposes and should thus be thought of as universal. As befitting its nature, it is presented without assurance regarding its prolonged validity or interim quality. Facebook is a registered trademark of Facebook Inc. and is used for descriptive purposes only. Other terms trademarked by Facebook may be used in this manuscript for descriptive purposes only. Trademarks that are mentioned are done without written consent and can in no way be considered an endorsement from the trademark holder.

Introduction

Let's begin by making a key observation about any business. The central item any marketer or business owner needs to have first and foremost in their mind is the *Cost of Acquisition* of a new customer. This is true no matter what you're selling. It's the one thing that all businesses have in common whether you're trying to sell a widget online, sell real estate, or running a mobile app business.

Its this fact alone which makes Facebook Advertising the ultimate marketing solution. Not only does Facebook Advertising give you a platform where you can drive down your cost of acquisition to minimal levels, it does so by letting you laser target your audience. Moreover, by using proper techniques you can improve your targeting dramatically over time.

Even better – once you learn the tricks of the trade you don't need to hire expensive and fancy consultants to do it. In this book we are going to teach you the exact steps we use in our own mobile advertising business – but what we teach applies to any business from encyclopedia sales to bringing new patients to a Chiropractor's practice.

Let's think about traditional advertising. You might consider running a radio advertisement for your real estate business. The ad will be somewhat effective, raising brand awareness. However the reality is 90% of the audience getting that message could care less. In truth its probably 99% who aren't interested. Using TV advertising you'd spend even more money for the same results.

What if you could use another approach, one that brought your customers into laser *focus*. Imagine being able to target women aged 35-54 with 2 children who have recently expressed interest in buying a house. Or imagine being able to target people that live within 25 miles of a certain zip code – or better – precise GPS coordinates.

And imagine that the more you ran your advertising campaigns – the lower the cost to acquire a new prospect.

Now you're starting to see the power of Facebook ads.

Even better, we can let the market speak to us. Using the techniques we are going to teach you in this book, you will be able to run low cost advertising and have Facebook filter out which ads work and which don't and have winning marketing campaigns in a matter of days.

OK enough with the hype. Lets dive right in and start learning the nuts and bolts of Facebook advertising.

Chapter 1: Creating Your First Ad

Before we learn the specific strategies that will make your Facebook ad campaigns bring you all the customers you've ever dreamed of at the lowest price, let's go through the mechanics of creating and running a Facebook ad.

The first step is to setup a Facebook page for your product or service. So where do you take care of all this? In case you don't know, the website where you'll go to access your Facebook Ads Manager is here:

https://www.facebook.com/business

Draw your attention to the very top of the web page. There you'll see a "create ad" button.

But before we go about creating an ad, you want to make sure you have a *Facebook Page* for your product or service. You don't have to even direct customers to the page but you do need to have one associated with your ad. In my case, I often use Facebook ads to get downloads for mobile games I sell. My ad actually takes the user to the download link for the game and not to the Facebook page, but I still need a Facebook page associated with the ad.

Creating Your Facebook Page

The website where you can go to create your Facebook page is here:

https://www.facebook.com/pages/creation/

Click on it and assuming you're signed into your Facebook account, you'll see something like this:

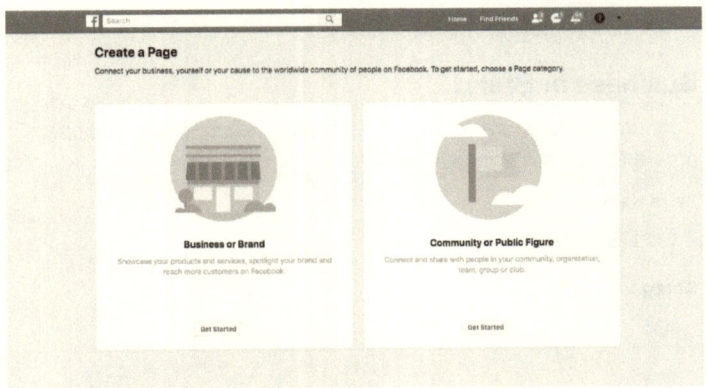

As you can see we can create a page for a community or public figure, but for our purposes we're interested in creating a *Business or Brand* page. So click *Get Started* under Business or Brand.

Facebook will ask you to name your page and then choose a category. You choose your category by typing in a description of your product or service and then choosing from one of the pre-defined categories that popup in their list. For this example, I am going to create Facebook page for an App I'm marketing called 777 Lucky Slots Casino. It's a game available in the Apple App Store. The closest categories I can find in their list are *Video Game*, and *App Page*.

Business or Brand

Connect with customers, grow your audience and showcase your products with a free business Page.

Page Name

777 Lucky Slots Casino

Category

App

Apparel & Clothing

App Page

Appliances

Appliance Repair Service

Apparel Distributor

Real Estate Appraiser

Book

Clothing (Brand)

Engineering Service

Men's Clothing Store

I decided to go with App Page as that seems a bit closer to what I need. When you've made your selection, click the *Continue* button.

Next, Facebook is going to ask you to upload a profile picture and cover photo to use for the page. You can skip these steps and do them later, but I'm going to use the App Icon and a screenshot from the game to serve these purposes. If you're a real estate agent (say), you would probably use your own photo for the profile photo and maybe a picture of a nice house for the cover photo. The cover photo is the image that will appear at the top of the page. The input screens for these steps look like this:

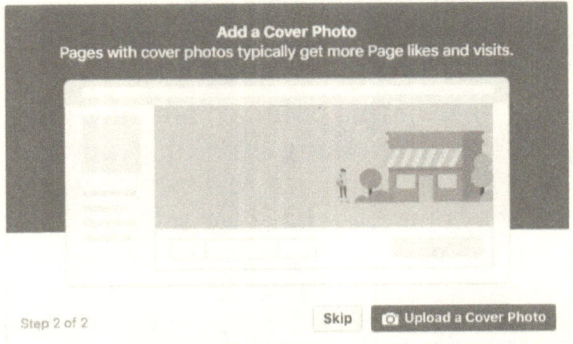

After I've uploaded my images, the basic setup of my page looks like this:

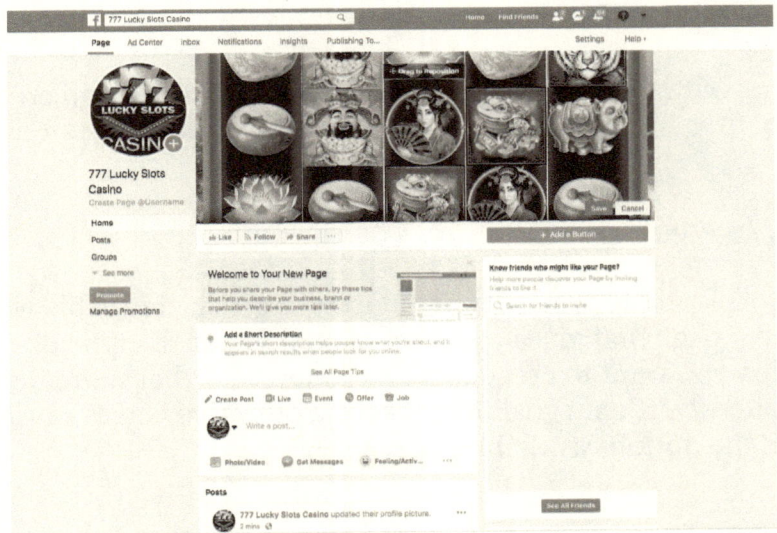

Note that in the lower right you will see a section of suggested Friends you might want to ask to like your page (for privacy reasons, I have greyed out that section of the page). Its probably worth asking some friends and family to like your page to make it look a little better, so that when your first prospects come to the page they'll see social proof that others have already liked the page.

Before doing that, however, your first item of business is to enter a brief page description where it says *Add a Short Description*. Don't be boring, you want to convey the purpose of the page while at the same time selling yourself. If you had a real estate business, maybe you'd put something like "Helping Houston Residents Find the Home of Their Dreams Since 2003".

While you're ready to go at this point, consider adding your first post to the page. It can be anything that will generate some interest from your prospects. For example, a real estate agent can post a picture of a home they currently have for sale, or one that recently sold if you're using the page to target people who want to sell their homes. In my case for a mobile game I'll put up a post about a current bonus or new game or description of an update available in the app. The page works just like the regular Facebook you're used to, so navigating the page once its created is easy and familiar.

Creating Your First Ad

With that out of the way, we're ready to push forward and create our very first advertisement. You'll create and manage your ads here:

https://www.facebook.com/adsmanager/

Simply click on the green *Create* button to get started. This will bring up a page that gives you a set of choices for the type of campaign you want to create. In this context, by that we really mean what your advertising goal or marketing objective is. Let's briefly go through the options available.

- Brand Awareness. Use this option to make prospects aware of your brand.
- Reach. A vague option Facebook provides, to reach as many customers as possible.
- Traffic. Use this if you're trying to use Facebook ads to drive traffic to your website. This assumes you have an off-Facebook destination where you want to send traffic.
- Engagement. This option is used for standard Facebook activities. For example if you're after page likes this might be an option to consider.
- App Installs. Used to specifically advertise mobile apps on Google Play or Apple's App Store.

- Video Views. Use this option to drive viewers of your video content.
- Lead Generation. Used to collect email addresses of prospects.
- Messages. Get prospects to use Facebook messenger or Whats App to send messages to your business.
- Conversions. Drive conversions.
- Catalog sales. Will show items from your catalog, targeting the audience you're advertising to.
- Store Visits. If you have a "brick and mortar" business, you can use this type of ad to encourage people to visit your physical location.

Obviously many of these choices are vague and there is also a great deal of overlap between them. For example, you might create a Facebook page for your brick and mortar location but use an "Engagement" campaign to drive Facebook users to like your page where they'll see the physical location of your store. And maybe you have coupons there visitors could redeem at the store. Some choices like lead generation, Catalog sales, and App Installs are more specific.

There are some important differences to note, however. For example, "Brand Awareness" isn't going to connect your Facebook page to the advertisement. Reach, however, will do so. An ad created for App Installs will include a download link to the app in the ad in addition to a link to the given Facebook page. All will have different suggestions for daily budgets and how you'll pay for the ad. We'll discuss some of the different ad types in more detail later, but for the sake of this presentation we will select *Reach* for our first ad.

The first thing to do is name your campaign. You will also note the possibility to turn on A/B testing, which we will discuss later. You can also optimize your budget across *ad sets*. This is important to note, as Facebook lets you create advertisements at the *campaign* level. You can have multiple *ad sets* within each campaign. If you turn on budget optimization and create multiple ad sets, Facebook will attempt to spend your money in such a way as to have your dollar spend generating the most results (whatever that result is defined to be, such as a page like or app install). So if you have three ad sets in one campaign, and one ad set is converting a lot more than the others, Facebook will try to drive more spending to the better campaign.

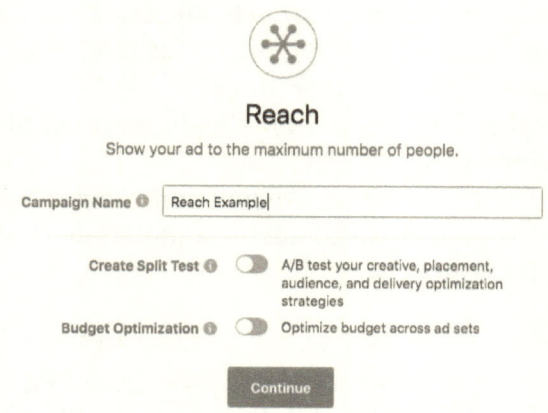

However, using the strategies we are going to teach in this book, we are going to do our split testing and optimization manually. That might strike you as odd but it will allow us to harness the power of Facebook ads more effectively and only takes a small amount of extra work. I also keep the structure of Facebook simple by putting one ad set with one campaign. We'll see the why and how of this later, but for the sake of our first example let's just forge ahead by clicking the *Continue* button.

When we do so, the first thing Facebook is going to ask us is which Facebook Page to associate with the ad. If you've created multiple Facebook pages, as I have for different apps in my companies portfolio, then you'll see a drop down list near the top of the page which allows you to select the page you want to use.

I've selected the Facebook page that I recently created for this example.

Page
Choose the Facebook Page you want to promote.

Facebook Page   777 Lucky Slots Casino

Right below Page, we'll see the first very important part of our Facebook ad – the Audience!

This allows you to select who will see your ad and where they are. Locations where you want to advertise are the first item of business. By default, it will have the country where you reside listed, which for me is the United States. By clicking on the name displayed in locations, you can bring up a map that you can use for more detailed targeting. The map works like any online map you're probably familiar with. So you can zoom in or out, and drag with the mouse to get to various locations. The map then allows pin dropping.

Typically, for mobile app installs I will target at the country level. I may even include multiple countries in the same campaign. Facebook allows you to type in a location which can be a city, country or whatever you might think of. Targeting can be quite specific but you'll have to experiment to find out if what you need is available. For example, I can type in Orange County to bring up several options. It even allows me to target John Wayne Airport in Orange County, California.

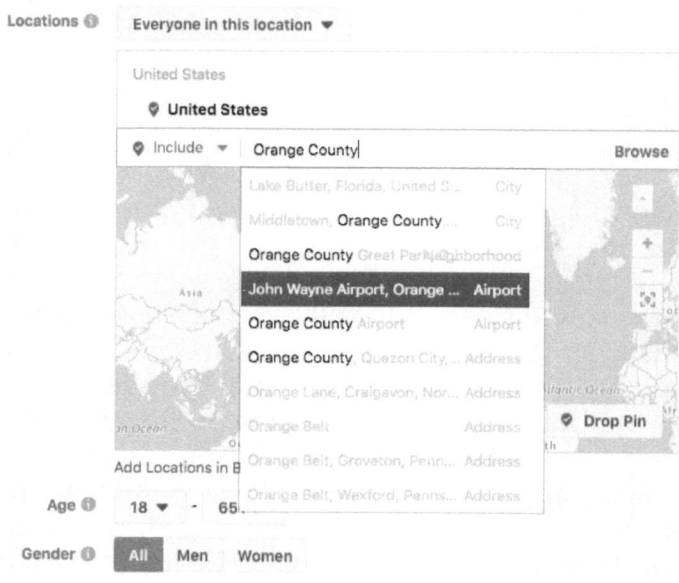

For my purposes, that's far too specific, so I will just go with Australia and the United States.

However before we move on, lets take a look at pin dropping with the map.
To select a location by pin drop, first click once with your left mouse button on *Drop Pin*. Then move your mouse to the location on the map where you want to drop the pin, and click once there. If you need to zoom in more before dropping your pin.

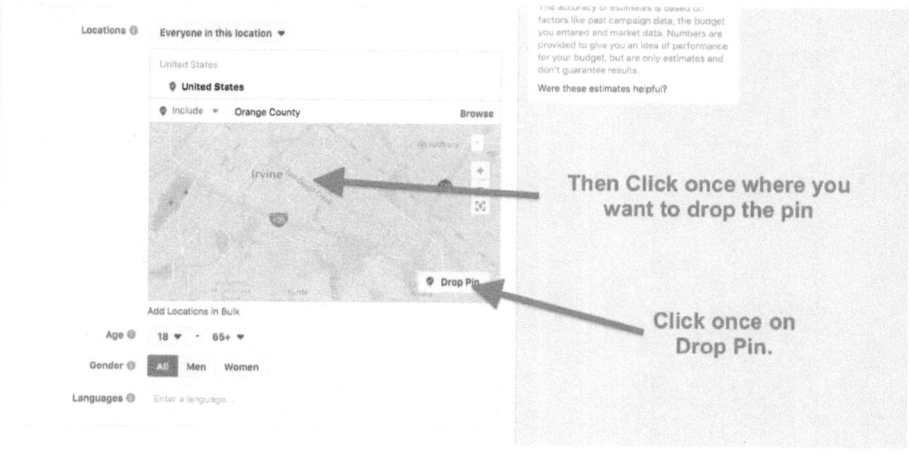

When the pin drop location is selected, Facebook will give you the coordinates of the location you've chosen, and the radius about those coordinates where your ad will show defaulting to a 10 mile radius. To change the distance, simply click on it and use the slider bar to increase or decrease the radius.

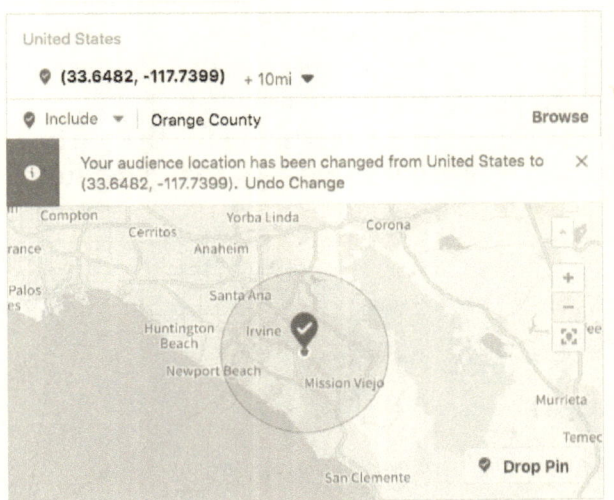

This level of location targeting might find many uses, for example if you're looking for store visits to your restaurant, you can target people that are within a certain distance of your location. For most applications however, you'll probably be targeting your ad locations simply by typing in the name of a country, state, or city.

At this point, you might have noticed that we glossed over the top of the Audience section where it says "Create New" or use a "Saved Audience".

The reason we're doing this is that we're assuming this is your first Facebook ad and that you don't have any saved audiences. We'll reserve discussion of these items for a future chapter, which covers the topic *Audience Insights*.

Age, Gender, and Language

The next item to note is the Age and Gender section. Properly selecting the age and gender of your target audience is going to be critical for successful advertising. However, if you are not sure and/or this is your first time advertising for the particular product or service, you can leave this section set to the defaults.

Unless you have something you already know to be gender or age specific, use the first campaigns you create to let the market speak. If you go with the defaults you'll be able to analyze your Facebook data you get on the ad after it starts running to see if you need to zoom in on certain demographics.

A note on age, the youngest age you can use at this time is age 13.

To target speakers of a specific language, you can type in what you want in the *Languages* text box. This will bring up a drop down list giving your selections. For example if you are advertising in Quebec, you might want to target English speakers in Quebec and so select English, or you might be advertising in French and so need to select French Canadian.

Detailed Targeting

Detailed targeting is where the real power of Facebook ads comes into play. Its so powerful we're going to devote an entire chapter just to this topic. What it allows you to do is zoom in on members of the audience that have expressed an interest in various topics by liking another product page, for example.

You can use detailed targeting to target multiple interests you want to filter down to in your audience. Typically I'll put between 10-20 selections. As an example, lets type in the word "Mac":

We could, for example, be marketing a new hamburger for our restaurant and want to target people who like to eat Big Mac sandwiches at McDonalds. Or we might have software made for Apple Mac computers, and so we can target owners of Macbook Pro computers, by selecting this from the list. It doesn't actually specify that the person has a Macbook Pro computer, rather it allows us to target people who've liked pages related to Macbook Pro computers or have "expressed an interest in" Macbook pro computers. So they are likely a Macbook pro user or looking at buying one. The targeting is not perfect, but by selecting it we've massively narrowed down our audience to desirable prospects if we're selling software that runs on a Mac computer.

You will notice that Facebook provides a popup for each item that tells you what the audience size is, along with the specific interest and what it means.

My experience is this kind of winnowing works very well. Remember when we talked about radio ads? If you buy ad time on the radio, you'll be spending a fortune to reach everyone within the listening area of the radio station. Chances are the vast majority of the people hearing the ad won't care, and it will be "in one ear and out the other". They might even mute the sound while your ad runs.

So while you'll reach a small number of your intended audience, you're mostly burning money. Using mac computers as an example, roughly 12% of the population uses mac computers. So if you run ads on the radio for your software, just on a random sample basis 88% of the audience hearing your ad isn't even a prospect.

In this case using Facebook ads it's the opposite. We can start off the bat by filtering out people who don't have mac computers. So we've trimmed our prospect base that we are advertising to down to that 12% of people who might actually be interested in our product. As you can imagine this will be far more effective not only in reducing your advertising costs per prospect but also in getting paying customers faster and more effectively.

Audience

On the right hand side, you'll see a sidebar item called *Audience Size*. The important item to note is *Potential Reach* which gives you a rough estimate of how many people will see your ad every day. Keep in mind this is an estimate and actual results may vary.

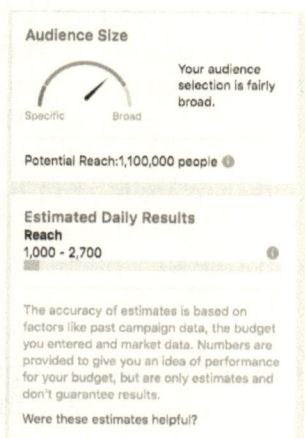

Placements

Next we'll look at placements. In a nutshell this is where in the Facebook empire your ad will run. Facebook recommends using Automatic Placements, but the reality is they are probably doing this to maximize their revenue. When it comes to managing your ads, whether you want to use Automatic Placements depends on many factors.

First lets examine the options we have. Generally there are four placement options, each with its own subcategories. These are:

- Facebook
- Instagram
- Audience Network
- Messenger

If you aren't sure, the best option is to start with automatic placements and then if necessary trim down to the ones that actually deliver for your product or service. However its important to note that not all placements will work for all products.

As an example, one of my own businesses is a mobile app business which markets slot machine casino games. I'm generalizing a bit here, but the core audience for these types of games can be described as:

- Female
- Age 35+
- Located in United States, Canada, Australia, and New Zealand

When it comes to placements, the key piece of data in my case is the age range. Why? Instagram users tend to be aged 18-29. Its not a hard and fast rule, but that's generally the case. So using Instagram in my case is a complete waste of time. It does drive some installs, but on a cost per unit basis, it's far more expensive than Facebook or the audience network. You'll have to look for similar situations for your own product or service although it's a general fact that Instagram users (this can apply to *Messenger* as well) tend to be younger while Facebook tends to target everyone.

Let's look at the breakdown inside each option. Starting with Facebook we have:

- Feeds
- Instant Articles

- In-Stream Videos
- Right Column
- Suggested Videos

As with using Instagram or not, you will want to look at your results from each of these items.

For Instagram we have:

- Feed
- Stories

Next there is Audience Network, mobile advertising. The options are:

- Native, banner, and interstitial
- In-stream videos
- Rewarded video

A "Native" ad is an advertisement that appears as a natural part of the content of a mobile application. A banner is like a web banner, it's a thin ribbon across the screen at the top or bottom. An interstitial is an obvious ad that pops up and takes up the users entire screen. Rewarded video is a video ad that gives the user the option of watching or not. If they watch, they get some reward inside the app. For example if it's a game the rewarded video will give the user some free coins for watching the video.

Finally we have Messenger:

- Inbox
- Stories
- Sponsored messages

General advice – if you have an audience with a lot of young people target all options. If you have an older audience, target Facebook and Audience Network. You may want to split up your advertising into two different campaigns targeting older and younger users. But test, test, test is always the rule – so if you aren't sure setup a campaign with automatic placements and let the results tell you what to do.

By moving your mouse cursor over a given selection, Facebook will show a preview to give an idea of what the ad looks like:

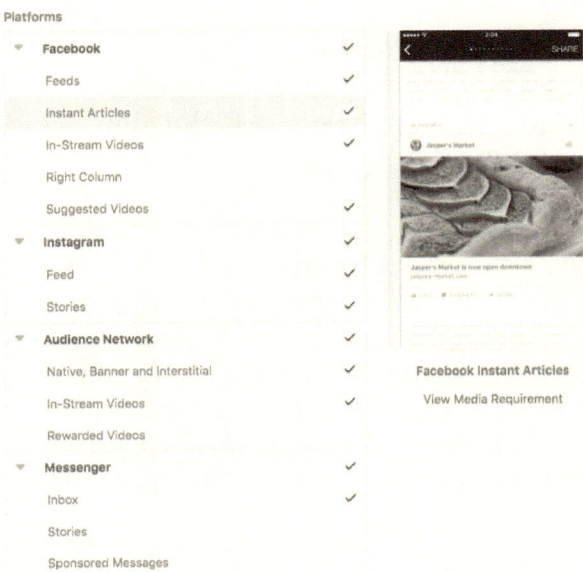

Budgeting

Now let's take a look at the Daily Budget. Facebook gives you a recommended daily budget. You'll find the amounts are not terribly high, but even so you'll want to start at a lower level than they recommend. We will talk about this more in the next chapter but if Facebook recommends a $40 budget, then start at $5. If it recommends $5, start at $2.50. You can increase your daily spend later. The key concept here however is you're going to test your ad out before upping the spend. To reach a large amount of customers with one ad campaign, you're going to need to have a much higher daily budget than they recommend.

You will see options for scheduling a start and end date or whether or not you want it to run continuously starting now. In the beginning, I recommend starting off with a run continuously option. Facebook ads can be turned on and off on the fly, so unless you have a specific need to run the campaign over a set number of days, then using the continuous option is better. I also recommend that you not run a targeted campaign that you want to go over a specific period until you've done ad testing. So if you want to have an ad targeting customers with your Christmas sale that runs Dec. 12-24, this type of schedule would be wise:

- Run a test ad from December 1-7.
- Collect data and refine until December 11.
- Based on results launch your schedule limited campaign December 12-24.

Many users will find time of day matters. In my case of slot casino apps, people download them for the most part during leisure times. Since most people work during the day, downloads drop off quite a bit between 9 AM and 5 PM. They are also low from 1 AM to 7 AM. So it doesn't make sense for me to be trying to show impressions during those time periods. With the vast majority of downloads running from 5 PM Eastern time to 1 AM Pacific time, I shut the ads off during other time windows, mostly during regular "business" hours.

Reach versus Impressions

Reach means that Facebook will try to show the ad to as many people as possible. You also have the option of targeting by *impressions*. This means that Facebook will try to show a lot of impressions to each individual its able to reach. If you think that a prospect seeing your ad repetitively is going to benefit you, then you'll want to try the impressions option.

Bid Strategy

Facebook defaults to "Lowest cost", attempting to deliver the most results for a given ad spend. However, you can set a Bid Cap. In my business, trying to drive mobile app installs, I can set a bid cap aiming for a given cost per install, say 75 cents. For our example of a *Reach* campaign, Facebook allows you to set a cap on the bid per 1,000 impressions. This is not a guarantee that Facebook can meet your specification. In my case if I put a bid cap of 85 cents, while it works sometimes and even gets me lower costs per install in some campaigns, most of the time Facebook tries to come close but still costs more than my target. That can still be useful strategy but the biggest drawback I've found is it slows down the campaigns. As a specific example, on a campaign with a $40 daily budget, but using the default lowest cost option, its guaranteed to spend the $40. But in cases where I've specified a cost per install goal even with a daily budget of $200 it actually spends less than $30 a day. You'll have to run tests to see what actually happens in your specific situation which may depend on what you're marketing and who your target audience is, but be aware that not using the default settings may slow your campaign down.

Identity and Creative Type

The next step is to select your "Identity". For a Reach campaign, this is already set to your associated Facebook page. For other types of campaigns you may have the option to select your identity here. Below this, you will see a set of creative options to use for your ad.

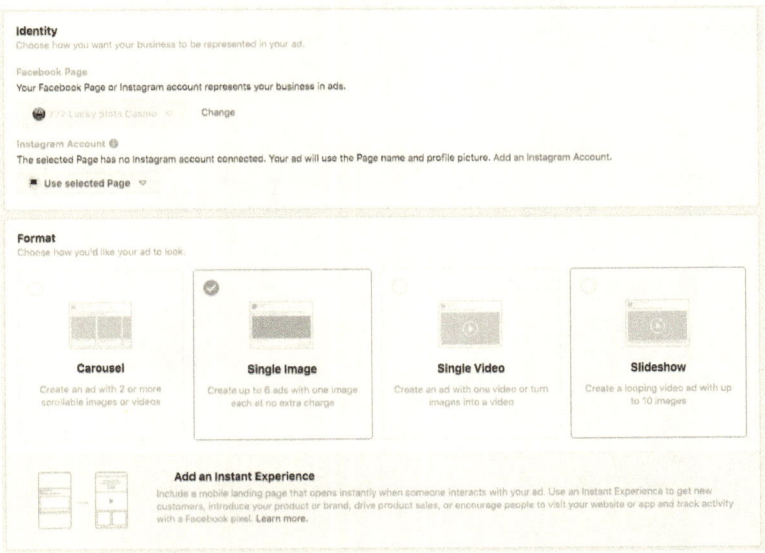

The options are self-explanatory, but a few notes based on previous experience.

- Facebook allows you to use stock images and videos, or upload your own.
- The image used for the ad (including the thumbnail for a video ad) cannot have text in the image. Limited amounts of text are allowed but may require Facebook review. It's a dumb rule, but it's the rule.
- Stock images and videos can work in some situations. However generally speaking your own image or video is going to work better. This is even true if its an amateurish effort. Customers can detect canned content. Not too mention, you're obviously better off showing *your* product in the ad.
- Video ads are by far the best.
- If you don't have the resources to make a video but have multiple still images, make a Slide show ad to approximate the benefits of a video ad.
- A Carousel is a good option if you have the right creatives.
- While not the best option, the default, Single Image ad can also be effective.

If you're not able to make your own videos, a step up from a slide show is to use the *Video Creation Kit*.

The Video Creation kit lets you make a professional "video" on the fly with a few stills and effects. You can select your own images/logo to use or use stock images.

Text for Your Ad

The next step is to set the text and headline(if applicable) for your ad. The important thing to remember here is that this is a *social marketing platform*. So don't just put in a boring line or statement:

- Call Jane Doe for your Real Estate needs
- For great Chiropractic Services, visit MyChiropractor.com

Although our goal is to either sell a product, get a page like or capture a lead, we want to take advantage of the social networking aspect of advertising by encouraging those who see the ad to interact with it in someway. Ideally they will like the post and share it with others, but you want to encourage people to comment on your advertisement.

A great way to do this is to ask a question. This will prompt viewers of the ad to comment, like the ad, and possibly share it. For example, if I am making a new ad for one of our casino games, I might want to list a benefit that a new user gets by downloading the game, such as free coins. I could say "Download Now and Get 10M Free Coins". However, its actually more effective to ask them a question. One good way to market to a primarily female audience (admittedly I am generalizing here, but on average it works) is to inject emotion into the ad. I could do that in this case by asking "How would it feel to receive 10 Million Gold Coins?" instead of just stating that they will receive a certain number of coins for signing on.

My ad might preview as something like this:

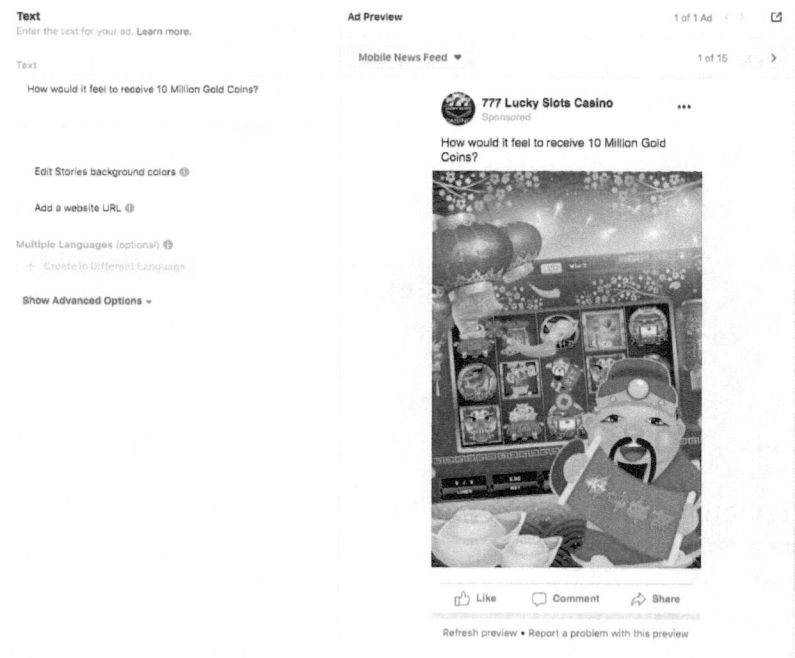

Now I've given viewers a reason to engage with the ad. Some will simply "Like" the fact I'm offering them free coins and therefore like the post. Others might share it with friends who also play casino games, and some will comment in response to the suggestion by actually answering the question. I could even improve this by incorporating some sensory qualities into the question, such as saying "glimmering Gold Coins" instead of just plain gold coins (even though no such real coins exist, I want them to exist in the prospects mind).

For our examples above, we might instead say:

- How would it feel to walk into your brand new three bedroom home in beautiful Irvine, California?
- Are you looking for the peace of mind that comes from owning your own home?

Its not always necessary to ask a question although in my experience questions are best. You can just paint a picture. For our chiropractor you might use "Imagine having a pain free back for the first time in months".

Note that some types of ads also have Headlines, which gives you another opportunity to provide some text to prompt the user to comment, share, or like the ad which is basically just another post in Facebook, albeit a paid one.

The final step is to confirm and submit your ad for "review" (which is probably done automatically by bots in most cases, unless there is a problem). If you have a small amount of text in your image, whether it's a still image ad or a thumbnail used to represent your video prior to the user hitting the play button, you might see this warning:

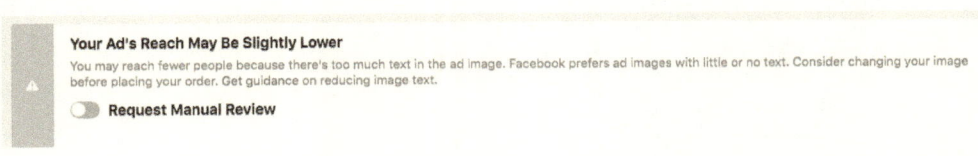

In most cases, you can just ignore the warning. If your text is incidental, as mine was in the ad shown above, it's not going to have any impact. In my opinion this is a silly requirement but Facebook makes the rules.

Now that we've learned the admittedly tedious and boring mechanics of setting up a Facebook ad, lets move on to learn about strategies for making your ads work for your business.

Action Point

What good is a practical book without exercises?

- Grab a piece of blank paper. Yes, paper and pencil – its better for the mind to actually write things out rather than relying on computer or "Siri".
- Write down your advertising goal. Is it to make a sale now, get a download, or simply drive brand awareness?
- Determine where your primary customers are.
- Write down all the specifics of your ad – budget, audience target, what type of ad you'll run (both Facebook category as

in lead generation or app install, and creative type – video, slideshow, still image or carousel).
- Make your creatives if you haven't already. If you truly don't have access to your own at this time then you are allowed to rely on Facebook stock images. Otherwise you might check Shutterstock.com or Dreamstime.com for a large selection of royalty free images and video.

Create your first ad and run it. Use a small budget since you're just learning ($5 or less per day).

Chapter 2: The First Path to Success -Hit it with Many Ads

We've noted that the power of Facebook ads lies in the ability to laser target your audience. Now we're going to take that observation a step further – by creating ads and then doing laser targeting in different directions. The more directions the better but obviously we don't have the time or resources to create hundreds of ads each day (although your large competitors might). The strategy involves the following steps:

- Create 1-5 different creatives to test. This can include five different videos, or some mix like 3 videos and 2 still shots.
- Break down your target audience in as many ways as you can think of.
- We'll be creating ads for each target and creative.
- Budgets will be set at basement lows.
- We'll let the ads run for three days.

Although most readers won't be running a mobile ad business, I'm going to use it as an example so you can see my real world results. Secondly the specific product isn't really relevant. The goal is to drive down your cost per acquisition of a new customer as far as you can.

What if you don't know your audience?

So lets start by doing some general audience analysis. In your own case, you may not know your audience yet. If that situation describes you, for now I suggest you read this chapter for information purposes with the intent on coming back to it later to take action. For now, create one ad and let it run to the most general audience you can so that you can collect data on who is most likely to respond.

Moving on, assuming that you know this information now, the first step is to create a listing of audience breakdowns. Using my example of casino ads I know the following bits of information:

- Slot players tend to be female, but are not exclusively female.
- Downloads by gender depend on theme. Therefore I will want to test different themes and possibly segment by gender.
- There are slot players worldwide, however the best markets for earning a profit from long term users are the United States, Canada, Australia, and New Zealand.
- Slot players are not exclusively but tend to be older than 35.
- Older audiences don't tend to use messenger or Instagram.

You may or may not be advertising a product or service that you can sell to a global audience. However you still may have location targeting, whether it's a city, state, or even neighborhood. Remember that we can target right down to a zone of a few miles around a specific GPS coordinate.

Tip: You may not want to limit yourself. For example, if you're a real estate agent in Phoenix, you might consider trying ads in New York. You could target users who've expressed an interest in selling or buying a home and who've also expressed an interest in Phoenix. Many of those people might actually be planning to move to Phoenix. Imagine how far ahead of the game you'd be targeting those people before they even get to Arizona, while your competitors are running around posting signs in the neighborhood?

So lets look at how I'm going to setup my ads. I begin by selecting *App Installs* when creating my campaigns. For you it might be something different like lead generation but the principles are the same for most campaigns. Our goal is to get the desired *result* at the lowest acquisition cost. The fact is since my apps are free to download, I'm really doing lead generation, and then a subset of those leads will play the game for more than a minute or two and spend money inside the game either by responding to advertisements in the game or buying in-app purchases.

The first obvious choice is to look at my different creatives. In my current example, I am marketing a slot casino game that has many different themed virtual slot machines inside the game. Most of them are "locked", requiring game players to reach certain milestones before being able to play them, but I've provided a few "unlocked" themes to entice users with different propensities to try out the game. For example:

- Chinese theme (appeals to male market more often than average)
- Egyptian theme (appeals to female market on more often than average)
- "Progressive" Jackpot (details not important if you don't know slots, key is this appeals – on average – to male users)
- Mayan theme (undetermined)

Right away we see opportunities to laser target our ads. In your case, if you're a real estate agent, you might have several homes for sale with different features that will appeal to different demographics in your target audience. Maybe you'll target families with children under the age of 18 living in the home with ads about being in a good school district. You might target older audiences with an ad for a different home and so on.

In my case, I created different videos for each free "unlocked" theme. For each creative, there are multiple ways to segment the ads. Remember the more ads the better. You want to segment in a way that you spend your daily budget in $5 increments. So if you are able to spend $100 a day for 3 days, you'll want to create 20 ad variations.

Going back to my examples, I can start with the Chinese theme video. Although I know from previous experience that on average it appeals more to male users, we want to follow the most important rule of all : *let the market tell us*. Therefore for the first three days I will set up ads using the Chinese video in the following manner, each with a $5 daily budget:

- Campaign #1: General, for all audiences 18+ on Facebook, Instagram, Audience Network, and Messenger.
- Campaign #2: Male audience. For males with slots, I will target 18+. Since the user base will include younger players, I'll target Facebook, Instagram, Audience Network, and Messenger.
- Campaign #3: Female audience. My experience is they tend to be older, so I will target 35+, and only show ads on Facebook and Audience Network.

For the testing phase, I will only advertise in the United States. After I've reviewed the performance of these ads, then I can expand to my other geos – Australia, New Zealand, and Canada.

Setting Your Goal

Obviously to determine whether an ad works or not you need a specific goal. For an ad spend of $5 per day we aren't going to get a large number of customers, but what we will get after three days is some data on click through rates, engagement, performance on different platforms (Instagram versus Facebook) and most importantly the *cost of acquiring a new customer*. For my business, this will be reported as cost per install and the target for me is around $1 or less. You need to be specific so rather than saying "around" I'll say $1.30 or less.

So there are two new rules you need to apply:

- Set a specific cost per result that you consider a success.
- After a three day run, any campaign that fails to meet your criteria gets turned off and you don't go back to it.
- If none of your campaigns meet your criteria, then you'll need to re-evaluate.

Laser Targeting the Laser Targeted Ad

Now at this point we've identified three campaigns to run. First I want to note that although Facebook lets you create multiple ad sets within a campaign, I tend to separate things out at the campaign level for simplicity.

In each case, we'll want to look at the *Detailed Targeting* of each ad we create. Using my example, my first set of ads is designed to show the video I made of the Chinese theme in my game. How can I use detailed targeting in my case? By using interests related to other Chinese themed slot games. Let's have a look. Doing some research I found a couple of large slot games in the App Store that have primarily Chinese themes. They are named "88 Fortunes" and "Fa Fa Fa Slots". Checking under Detailed Targeting → *INCLUDE people who match at least ONE of the following* I was able to find that people who have liked both apps make up large Facebook audiences (more than half a million each). So I set these up under my detailed targeting:

> Detailed Targeting INCLUDE people who match at least ONE of the following
>
> Interests > Additional Interests > FaFaFa Slots
> **FaFaFa Slots**
>
> Interests > Additional Interests > Slots 88 Fortunes
> **Slots 88 Fortunes**
>
> Add demographics, interests or behaviors   Suggestions   Browse
>
> Exclude People or Narrow Audience
>
> ✓ Expand interests when it may increase app installs at a lower cost per install.

In the first couple of days of your campaign, it's not strictly necessary to do this. However you seriously increase the odds of acquiring customers and driving your cost per result down by targeting relevant interests. By limiting my audience to people who've previously played Chinese themed slot machine games, I've upped the odds that they are going to respond positively to my video ad which shows another Chinese themed slot.

It's a simple rule of marketing. Find what people like – and give it to them.

Now my game isn't entirely Chinese themed like these are, but that doesn't matter. Most slot players enjoy variety so I built my game with variety, but by focusing on the theme I can use that as a hook to draw in a new customer.

Now how can this work in your case? If you aren't entirely sure try hitting the Browse button.

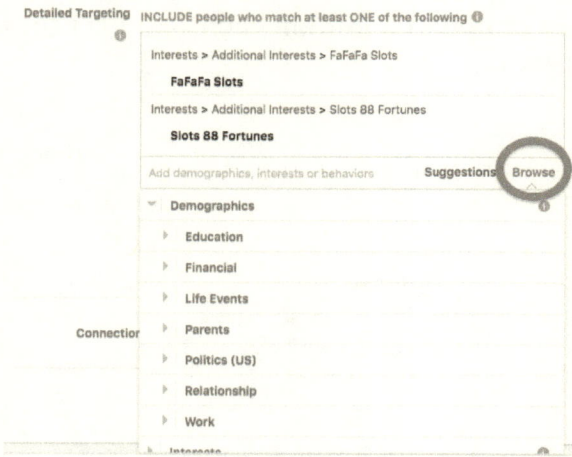

This will allow you to select people by various categories who may be interested in your product or service. Using suggestions you can check for specific interests or brand names that may have a presence on Facebook. The slot games I selected for example, have Facebook pages so were available under "suggestions". So basically I am marketing to *their* Facebook audience. However, not all Chinese themed slots have a Facebook presence. But you have to go with what's available, and generally speaking there is more than enough available.

We'll be talking about how to create and save audiences ahead of time in a future chapter. But you can do both – use a saved audience or go on the fly when creating your ads.

Quiz Question: Can you think of other ways to make more ads from what we've discussed so far?

The answer is : YES!

Using still screenshots, I can create two more Chinese themed ads for my game. Oh wait, I can create three:

- Slide Show
- Mix of video and stills in a carousel
- Single image ad

So now I can in theory at least create three more ads for each of my three general campaigns with the Chinese theme. The goal is to find out what works the best. Maybe more than one "works" the only way to find out is to test, test, and test some more.

If we decided to go with the mix of slide show and stills in addition to our original video, we're up to 12 total ads.

We could even break it down further. It may be the case that users of "88 Fortunes" really like my game, while users of "Fa Fa Fa slots" aren't interested. So we could break down ads to show to each target.

You won't necessarily want to do all this breaking down, but the key is to think about what possibilities you do have. Remember set your budget and divide by 5, that's how many ads you want to run in your test period. So if you only have a $20 daily budget then make 4 ads with key variations to find the best ad that works.

Your key variations are:

- Location of your audience
- Age range
- Gender
- Interests under detailed targeting
- Creative used in your ad

If you're selling shoes nationwide in the United States, maybe different ads will work in Texas and California. To find out, make ads to target each separately and both at the same time and find out what works.

You'll also want to consider placements as we've already discussed:

- Try advertising on Instagram, and not advertising on Instagram
- You might also try selecting among individual choices within your placement (example, try advertising on Facebook Feeds, but not Suggested videos). However I haven't found that level of detailed drill down to be productive.

A special side note for those requiring some kind of download or selling software – be sure to check required operating system and if you have a large download, require Wifi connection since many users will be using Facebook on mobile.

Action Point

In the last chapter I asked you to create a single ad. Now think about 3 new variations you could use to retarget the ad to a different demographic. Then run all 4 ads together for 3 days to gather your results with a maximum budget of $5 for each.

Chapter 3: Analyzing Ad Performance

We've seen that the best way to approach Facebook ads is to create a large number of variations to our ad and run them all for a few days. After we've done so, we need to look at what actually happened and determine what to do next.

The general idea is to find out which ads don't work and SHUT THEM OFF. Since you've already built in lots of variations ahead of time you don't need to waste time tweaking them after the fact to find out if minute changes will improve the performance of your ads.

So how do you go about doing this? Its pretty easy – just go to your Facebook ads dashboard. There you'll see all your campaigns. Again, this is just me – but I keep it simple by keeping one ad per campaign so I don't have to do any drilling down. I am going to shut most of them off anyway but it lets me see at a high level what's working and what's not. You don't have to do it this way of course, you can navigate all the intricacies of the Facebook setup if that's your preferred way of organizing things. In other words, I could have one campaign targeting women, then have ads sets inside the campaign targeting Chinese themed ad, Egyptian themed ad, etc. – but instead I am breaking things down at the campaign level.

In any case, lets look at some of my results for a couple of weeks of advertising:

So I got 929 installs on $1,319.58 of ad spend. If you're looking to smart small, don't be put off – like I said you start with what budget fits your situation. Of course some others are laughing at how little I spent.

The key here however isn't the absolute amount spent, but how am I doing as far as achieving my goal of paying $1.30 or less per install? Assuming I didn't make any dopey mistakes with the calculator I'm at $1.42 per install overall. Its not hugely off but its too high for me to make a profit. But as you can see I've created a whole bunch of campaigns so the task now is to look at which ones worked and which ones didn't work.

Facebook allows you to look at the data in a myriad of ways, something we'll talk about in the next chapter. The default is *Columns: Performance*. The nifty thing about the default arrangement is it gives you a column in the middle labeled *Cost per Result* – so I can zoom in on that and see what campaigns worked and which didn't. As I do this I am going to show you some other ways that I varied my campaigns.

Here is a zoom in on what I've got:

Cost per Result
$2.08 Per Mobile App Install
$1.75 Per Mobile App Install
$2.05 Per Mobile App Install
$1.53 Per Mobile App Install
$2.15 Per Mobile App Install
$0.96 Per Mobile App Install
$0.75 Per Mobile App Install
$0.82 Per Mobile App Install

Key observation? Several campaigns met my target and did so in stellar fashion. Some others were way off. The one at the top, at $2.08 per install, is painful. That one was definitely shut off after a few days. Let's talk about the settings for that campaign.

The first thing to note is the daily budget. The recommended budget was $40, but breaking with my usual procedure I went with a $30 budget to start with (I do recommend you start with $5). Nonetheless, keep that $30 daily budget setting in mind.

Second, I went with automatic placements. For app installs the default setting is "Lowest Cost". I went with this rather than trying to aim for a target cost.

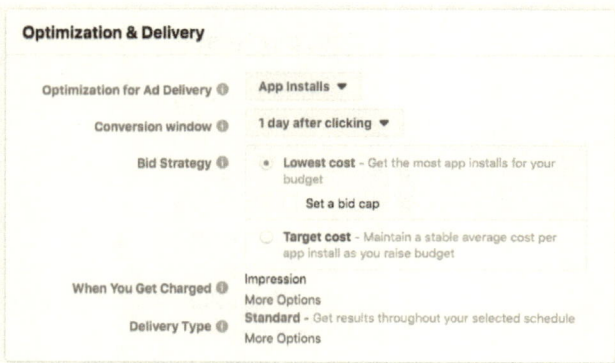

We can take a quick look at some of the data to determine why this ad might not have been as effective as we'd like (it did deliver 99 installs, but they were too expensive). You can take a look at some charts and graphs Facebook will display for you by clicking on "View Charts" for the Ad Set.

This will allow you to quickly glance at performance, demographics, and placement.

For performance, we'll be able to see how cost per result and number of results changed over time. The ad actually shows some favorable trends. Over the course of five days, the number of results per day went from 12 to 28. Over the same time period the cost per result dropped from $1.72 to $1.58. That's good of course, but not good enough. As we'll see in a bit rather than dealing with trying to tweak this ad into performing, our procedure of creating multiple ads setup differently allowed me to simply pick out the performing ads and just shut this one off.

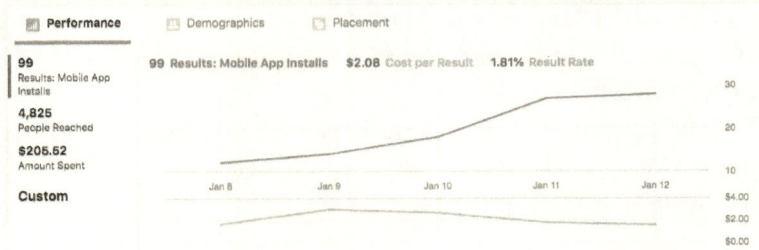

Nonetheless lets keep looking it over to see what information we can glean from the data. For this ad I mixed men and women and initially had it set for all adults 18 and over. Something interesting is that the lowest cost per result occurred for women aged 35-44 at $0.97 cents per install. For women 65+, there were far more installs but the cost per install was much higher at $2.01.

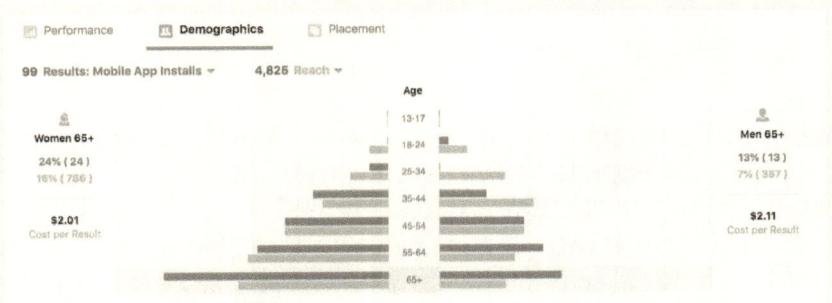

This tells me that I might want to *try* a campaign focusing only on women aged 35-44. Of course its not a guarantee it would work, but its something to look at.

You can see that overall there is less interest from men, however there is enough to warrant keeping them in the advertising loop. We don't want to leave any dollars on the table even if the demographic is smaller.

The third major item we can look at in the charts is placement. Predictably, Facebook got us a lot more results than instagram. This app had not been targeted by placement.

Key findings:

- On the audience network, the cost per result was $3.23.
- On Facebook, cost per result was $1.96 – a significant improvement.
- On Instagram, cost per result was $1.58. Better still but the reach was much smaller (as expected).
- Messenger got no results.

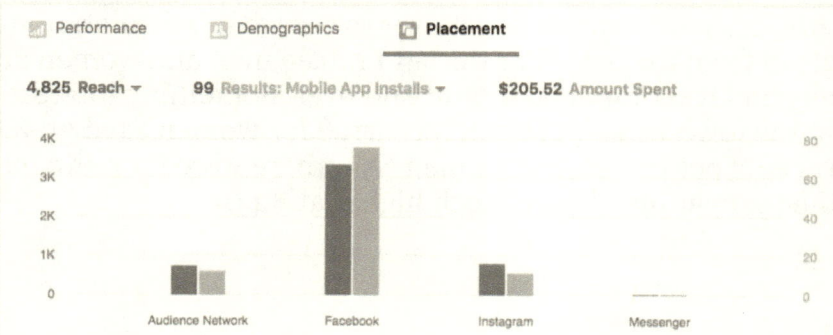

From our key findings, the audience network is not worth having as $3.23 is *way* too expensive for my purposes. As this was my first campaign for this particular application, I shut off the audience network in all future campaigns. I also shut off Messenger, since Facebook was not able to even show impressions. That might have been due to the interests I had used in detailed targeting – simply put none of those users are even on Messenger. So why waste time targeting it?

In any case, due to the overall cost per result, I immediately shut this ad off. I can do this because of my technique of hitting the market with lots of ad variations right away to find out what works. Lets look at one example that worked and maybe see some differences that produced these results.

Here we see a campaign called CPI Egypt got 85 installs at $0.82 cents each – far below my target of $1.30.

Campaign Name	Results	Reach	Impressions	Cost per Result
AU Only High Budget App installs - Copy	113 Mobile App Installs	1,449	2,404	$0.75 Per Mobile App Install
CA/UK Only High Budget App installs - Copy	30 Mobile App Installs	654	1,073	$0.81 Per Mobile App Install
CPI App installs Egypt	85 Mobile App Installs	2,765	3,152	$0.82 Per Mobile App Install

For this campaign, I actually got $0.75 app installs on Facebook — for me this is the road to profitability. So we drill down in the data — and find what works. In this case Instagram only produced 7 results, confirming the observation I shouldn't use Instagram for the best results from my ads (your results may vary). This time our app installs on the Audience Network had a cost per result of $0.97. Far better than previously, but the overall picture here is to do the following:

- Remove Instagram and Audience Network from the placements of this ad.
- Scale it up.

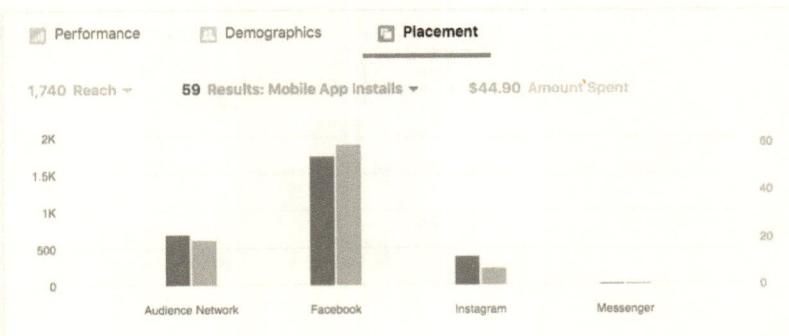

This ad actually had a higher daily budget. I had set the budget to $40, which was the suggested budget of Facebook.

```
Budget & Schedule

Daily Budget    $40.00
                $40.00 USD
                Actual amount spent daily may vary.

Start Date      Sunday, January 13, 2019 at 10:15 AM
                Pacific Time

End Date        • Don't schedule end date, run as ongoing
                ○ End run on:

Ad Scheduling   • Run ads all the time
                ○ Run ads on a schedule
```

But truthfully that's not really relevant. Nor is the specific ad creative I used (Egypt theme, turned out both that and Chinese worked). The key to success for this ad was I told Facebook to hit a specific target per install:

```
Optimization & Delivery

Optimization for Ad Delivery   App installs ▼
Conversion window              1 day after clicking ▼
Bid Strategy                   ○ Lowest cost - Get the most app installs for your
                                 budget
                               • Target cost - Maintain a stable average cost per
                                 app install as you raise budget
                                 $0.90           per app install
                                 Your current cost per app install based on a 1 day
                                 click conversion window is $0.87. Learn more

When You Get Charged           Impression
                               More Options
Delivery Type                  Standard - Get results throughout your selected schedule
                               More Options
```

I set my target to $0.90 – and Facebook actually beat it.

So for me this campaign's a keeper. There are a couple of ways we could proceed. Currently, the campaign is targeting men and women, all age groups, in USA, Canada, and Australia. I would scale up the daily budget to see if Facebook extends the daily reach, but I could also simply duplicate the campaign and turn it into several more, each with the same settings targeting a specific demo.

In fact I'll show you why I won't scale up the budget in a moment. For now, lets think of ways we can break this out into several ads:

- Create duplicate ads one each for USA, Canada, and Australia.
- Break each of those down into one targeting women, and one targeting men.
- Break those down into one with 18-44 targeting Facebook+Instagram, and one targeting 45+ for Facebook only.

So you can see how we start with one ad that works –and appears to do so fairly well across the geos and demography – and turn that one ad into 12 different ads. With literally tens of millions of people playing slot games on the iPhone and iPad, it will take a long time for these small ads to run their course, but they'll each deliver me a good dose of daily low cost customers. As each variant of our successful ad runs, we can analyze it for further refinements to drive our costs down even more (for example, maybe after splitting them up Instagram works more for women, not for men).

I've also learned a lesson for my case (your results may vary, but test it). In my case specifying a cost per result I want works better than letting Facebook try to drift toward the lowest overall cost.

Second, daily budget doesn't matter when I use those settings. We can check another campaign I've set up in a similar fashion using the Chinese themed ad.

Quick Aside: If you have a campaign that's working, move your mouse over it and click on Duplicate. You can create an exact copy of the campaign and then open it up to edit and make needed changes.

Getting back to the issue of daily budget, it turns out that on a campaign setup almost exactly the same way the daily budget was much higher at $200. Both campaigns produced about the same number of results per day.

Most important observation, neither spent the specified daily budget. Setting a budget at $200 when specifying the cost per result I want actually only resulted in it spending $25-30 per day. This could be because Facebook is working hard to hit my target so isn't proceeding fast in delivering impressions (although I told it my cost per result target, I am still bidding on impressions).

Action Point

Assuming that you've set up at least 3-4 different campaigns and let them run for a minimum of three days, take a look at your cost per result whatever that is and your overall data for cost over time, daily spend, demographics and placements as discussed in this chapter. For campaigns that are way off target, simply shut them down. If the campaign is close but not quite where you want it to be, refine your targets or change placements and demos. For campaigns that worked well, you can test raising the budget or creating duplicates to increase your daily customer acquisition numbers.

Chapter 4: Data Breakdowns

At this point it's a good idea to dive down even deeper. It's shocking how much data Facebook provides on your ad performance. First lets take a look at how you can organize what Facebook is showing you on the main screen.

First, if you click on *Columns*, you'll see several options available. The default setting is *Performance*. This shows you basic information about your campaign like Amount Spent, Reach, and Cost per Result.

If we select Delivery, we'll see some important items like Reach, Frequency, Cost per 1,000 People reached, Impressions, and CPM (Cost per 1,000 impressions). *Frequency* is the number of times a given individual sees your ad (on average). For my example ad, I have a frequency of 1.55, so some people saw the ad once and some saw it 2 or maybe 3 times.

In mobile advertising CPM is an important metric on most ad networks. For my ad I have a CPM of $42.47. Quite frankly in most circumstances this would be outrageously high! On Ad networks that specialize in running only on mobile, for my application I would bid a CPM of $12-16. So why bother with paying such a high price?

The answer is in the results.

Typically, on a mobile advertising network, a good performance a click through rate would be 12% and an install rate (the number of installs as a percentage of clicks) would be 15%. So for 1,000 impressions, you'd get 18 installs. For this particular campaign there were 2,165 impressions. This would deliver 39 installs.

So what did I get on Facebook? I got 96 installs in 2,165 impressions. Just about 2.5 times as many installs!

To get the number of clicks, we select Columns:Engagement. Doing that for my campaign I find there were 149 clicks with a cost per click of $0.62. The click through rate was 6.9%, a bit on the low side. However where Facebook delivers is by providing clicks that are customers ready to act. Remember out of those clicks I got 96 installs, that's an install rate of 96/149 *100 = 64.4%. This is a very high rate far higher than I could obtain with regular ads.

If you're running video ads, selecting Columns:Video Engagement gives you a large amount of detail on your ad. The information may or may not be useful to you, in my case I'm not necessarily interested in how many seconds a person watched the video. That doesn't necessarily give me all the information I need. My video ads are 30 seconds long. Now it might be the case that a prospect spends 10 seconds watching the ad, and that's all they need to install it. People watching the video all the way through might not even download the app. The reason is they might have needed more "convincing" and kept watching the video hoping something would come along to close the sale, and maybe it never does.

But the fact is there really isn't any way to know as Facebook doesn't give this information. In your case it might be different because you might have key information at some point in your video. If the information is shown halfway through the video, you'll be interested in the fraction of watches at 50%.

Tip: Keep your videos shorter, rather than longer. If you can fit your video into 15 seconds that's best, but 30 seconds is good. These days its not a great idea to have a longer video but that may depend on your specific product or service.

To see how many page likes, comments, and reactions your post has generated, select *Columns: Engagement*.

Breakdowns

Let's take a closer look at how you can use *Breakdowns* to examine the data from your campaigns. In my case, there are two important items of interest:

- Type of device used (since I'm advertising on mobile)
- Time of day

First, I'll go back to Columns:Performance. Next, I select *Breakdown: Conversion Device*. I can find this under *Breakdowns:BY ACTION*. Since its telling me "*Conversion* Device" its going to break down device by installs, and not by impressions. To view impressions I'd have to look at *BY DELIVERY*.

For this campaign, I found that there were 73 installs on iPhones and 22 on iPads (with 1 listed mysteriously as "other").

Conversion Device: iPhone	73
Conversion Device: iPad	22

That might not seem unusual to you, but to me its an odd standout. The reason is that historically on my slot games I've seen installs breakdown 52% iPad and 48% iPhone. The reason is that slots are more suited to play on iPads, so that's what most slot players do. That's a tip that something might be amiss. To double check, I'm going to take two steps. The first is to simply check where the impressions are shown, so as noted above I'll open the Breakdowns drop down menu and click on BY DELIVERY and then select Impression Device. When I do this I see that for the iPad, the reach was 389 and the impressions were 573. On iPhones the reach was 1,023 and the impressions were 1589.

Why this is so isn't immediately obvious and for various reasons I'm not sure it's important (more on that in a moment). It may result from people preferring to use Facebook on their iPhones. In fact chances are this is the case. At home you might be more inclined to even use your Desktop to check Facebook, but throughout the day you're certainly more likely to be looking at Facebook on the most portable device, which is the iPhone.

This begs the question, can I up my daily installs and drive costs down by advertising specifically to iPad users? That's not immediately clear but that's the second step I'm going to take – the best arbiter of the truth in business is what the market tells you. And in this case there is only one way to know for sure – run the ads on iPad only and see if the results are better.

However another piece of data indicates that might not produce better results. It's not always the case but chances are iPad users also have iPhones. The piece of information I'm noting is that nowdays Apple automatically installs an app you download to one device to all of your devices. So if someone is browsing Facebook on their phone, they might see the ad and like the app, and decide to install it. Then its automatically installed on their iPad.

The discrepancy with historical data could be explained by slot players getting on their iPads to specifically look for slot apps, which they'd prefer to play on their iPads.

OK so how does this result apply to you or more general cases? You will want to check your results by device for any type of ad. Suppose that you're running an ad to generate leads that you have sign up for your email list. You might find that older users aren't comfortable signing up on iPhones even though younger users are. So you might use that information to create a desktop only ad targeting your older demographics. Or maybe you're running ads on desktop and mobile, but you can use these breakdowns to check performance by device and maybe you find people aren't responding on desktop or vice versa, so you'll need to adjust accordingly. Maybe a general ad is showing on Android and Apple devices, but your conversion rate on Android is dismally low. In that case you could restrict your ad to only show impressions on iPhones.

In my case I've found Breakdown by Time of Day very helpful. What you want to select for in most cases is *Time of Day (Viewer's Time Zone)*. The relevant piece of data is what time the user sees the ad in their zone, not what time the ad is displayed where you are.

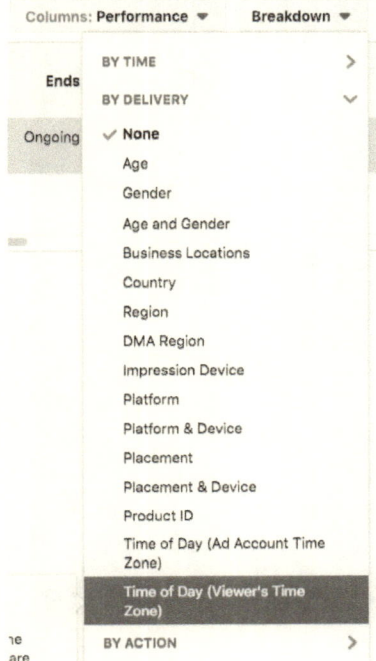

What I found for my own particular data is that my installs started picking up around 3 PM in the afternoon (user time) and lasted through midnight, after which time they died off. As noted in a previous chapter during most of the workday there were very few installs.

With this information in hand, I can manually turn ads on and off to maximize productive use of my impressions. I'd suggest giving an hour window, so I shut them off around midnight and then turn them back on maybe an hour early, about 2 PM to make sure they are ramped up and showing by 3PM.

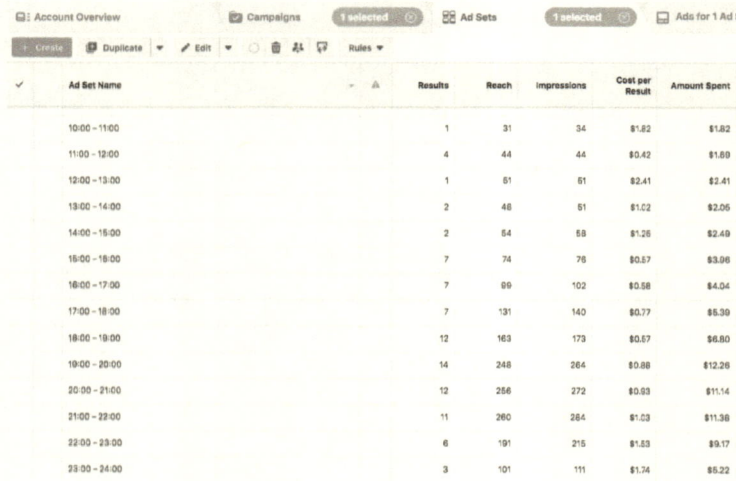

Chapter 5: Audience Insights

An important tool to use when developing your advertising campaigns is Audience Insights. We can access it from the menu, third item from the top:

Audience insights gives you a place to study the market and build and save audiences to use in your ad campaign. When you first open it the default setting is "Everyone on Facebook". If you've built up a substantial following on your Facebook page, you might want to analyze them as well. You would do this in order to market to a subset of your overall audience.

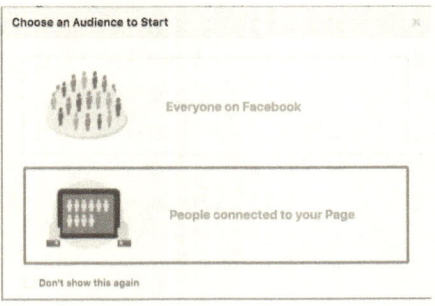

On the left side of the screen, you'll find the tools used to filter down your selection by demographics, interests, and location. It's nice to setup audiences prior to running your ad campaigns. There is also a great deal of information available here which you can't access when creating your ads.

So for the sake of example, let's start with the entire Facebook audience in the United States. You'll see a screen that looks something like this:

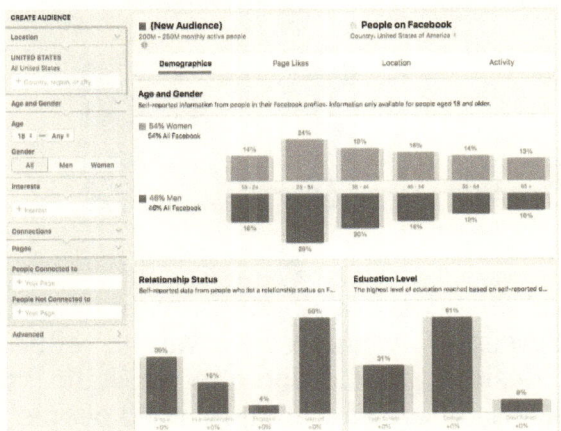

It doesn't include the entire population, but at 200M- 250M it's a huge fraction. The first things you might notice are that its skewed toward women at 54% and toward college educated people at 61% as compared to the general population (In the general population, something like 32% have a college degree – although Facebook doesn't make it clear if these are college graduates or "some college" + college graduates).

A nice feature of Audience insights is we can start targeting by simply clicking on the charts. So if I want to target only married people with college degrees, I just click with my mouse on both respective bars in the Relationship Status and Education Level charts. When I do this, the screen changes to this, and my audience size has been reduced to 30-35M users.

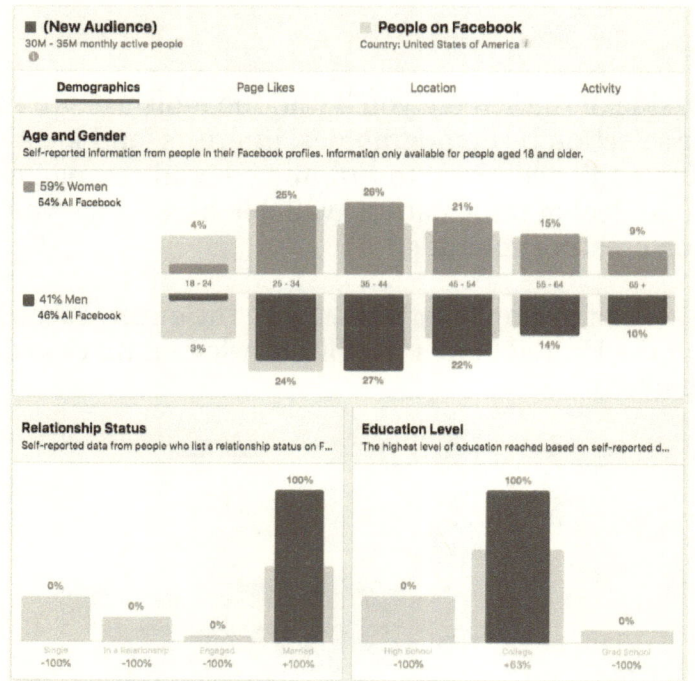

Facebook indicates selected demographic characteristics by marking the in green. Now suppose we want to refine our audience even further. If desired, you can zoom into specific locations. So if we wanted to select college educated, married people from Dallas, Texas, we could turn our attention to the Location box in the upper left and simply type it in:

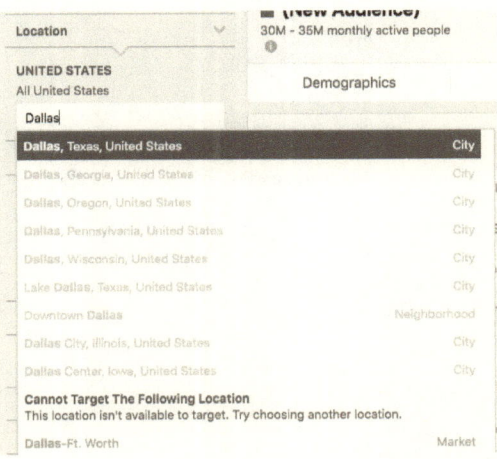

However, we might wait on that as zooming into a specific location can end up hiding a great deal of information from us. First lets click on the *Page Likes* tab at the top instead. When we do this we find some important information about our user base.

The top page like for married people on Facebook with college educations is *Dave Ramsey*. Looking at the table of page likes, toward the bottom of the tab, we notice it has an *Affinity score* of 24. That means the audience we've selected is 24 times as likely to like the Dave Ramsey page as compared to the general Facebook audience.

If you don't know who Dave Ramsey is, he is a financial coach/guru that helps people get out of debt. Its not too surprising that married people with college degrees – people who might have a lot of debt and financial problems –might be interested in Dave Ramsey. Of course it might be surprising that it's the top choice among page likes.

Suppose that you had an information product you were selling on financial management. By using this tool, you've found an audience you can target – we could return to the left side of the screen and look under *Interests*. Here we can filter out our audience in the same way that we could with *Detailed Targeting* when creating an ad.

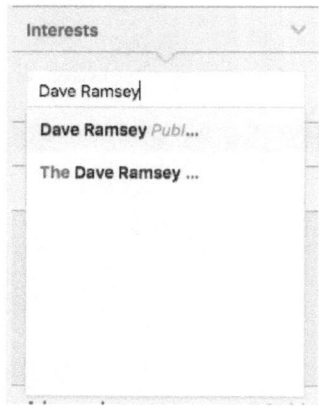

Doing this massively constrains our audience size – but if we have a get out of debt product to sell that people seeking Dave Ramsey's advice might be interested in – it's a well focused audience that is a good start for an advertising campaign. Our audience size is now just 1.5M.

For example, you could save this audience and make a short video (30-90 seconds) having one or two people talking about how your product helped them get out of debt (with maybe some soft piano music playing in the background). In your text you could make a time limited offer for a lead generation campaign, where you get people to sign up for your email list or for a webinar.

By "zooming in" with adding "Dave Ramsey" to the interests of our audience, you'll find that the page likes have changed. Now we see this:

Page Likes
Facebook Pages that are likely to be relevant to your audience based on Facebook Page likes.

Page	Relevance	Audience	Facebook	Affinity
Rachel Cruze	1	79.2K	250.4K	459x
Dave Ramsey	2	1.1m	3.8m	424x
Fierce Marriage	3	68.2K	475.2K	208x
Living Well Spending Less	4	84.1K	663.3K	184x
Lysa TerKeurst	5	134.6K	1.1m	171x
Jen Hatmaker	6	83.1K	722.5K	167x
Living Proof Ministries with Beth Moore	7	77.6K	699.1K	161x
Money Saving Mom	8	81.8K	830K	143x
Matt Walsh	9	63.7K	679.8K	136x
Chonda Pierce	10	66.7K	725.5K	134x

See More

The top of the page likes is now Rachel Cruz. Who is that? Click on it to find out. No surprise here — she's another debt guru. Our audience is 459 times as likely as the general Facebook audience to be interested in Rachel Cruze.

That is such a huge result — if I were marketing a get out of debt product I'd pause and take some time to study Rachel Cruze to figure out how I could tailor my product to the audience or at least tailor the advertising campaign to the audience.

- Take some time to watch videos posted on her Facebook page.
- Find out what she's selling.
- Jump on Amazon to check out books she's selling and specifically what they're about.
- Look for her unique selling proposition. How can you compliment it?
- Then tailor your ad to this.

Just looking at her post I took a screen shot of here, you might think of an ad with the title "Seven lies people believe about Debt". Or use the text field to ask a question – *What lies do you believe about getting out of debt?*

As you can see Audience Insights is a literal treasure trove of advertising information. We can use this information to literally customize our ads ahead of time to the audience! Have you ever imagined such marketing power before? Remember the old adage of marketing is find out what people want, and give it to them. Facebook gives us the first step – it makes it easy to find out what people want by researching what they're already looking at online to solve their problems. All you have to do once you have this information is tailor your communications in your Facebook ads to offer them the same thing, with your own unique selling proposition. Hopefully you've already developed a good product to do so, but I am sure you are noting the power of Audience Insights to help you brainstorm new products as well.

You could probably do very well stopping here – but you can do more. We can go back and check all of the page likes to learn more about their audience. I noticed in the list one of the top page likes was *Fierce Marriage*. That sounds like some kind of Christian group to me and clicking on it that's exactly what we find:

I'd call this insight secondary. We could target our audience even more strongly by putting a Christian element in our advertising or product. However its safe to assume that while the audience is more Christian than average, followers of Dave Ramsey and Rachel Cruze aren't necessarily evangelical Christians.

But frankly this sounds like an opportunity for A/B testing. If I had a get out of debt product I felt was of interest to the demographic we're studying, then I'd design one ad with the Christian element and one without the Christian element. Then we can compare results. Its possible both will deliver. Also we can use the results from our campaigns to build two new, laser focused audiences that are receptive to our products.

Clicking on the Location tab we can glean a lot of other useful information. This can give us a list of cities we might specifically target in our advertising campaigns. However, in this case the locations are such a small proportion it doesn't seem to warrant such an approach. You'll have to check in your own research what the numbers are, but here the top city is listed as Birmingham, Alabama.

Given the two main factors we've seen so far – married people in debt + Christian – that might not be much of a surprise that many of the cities are located in the south. However clicking on the bar chart for Birmingham we see that it only makes up 0.2% of our selected audience.

For me, that tells me its not worth targeting any further by location.

On the other hand, if you had selected a certain demographic and found that 10% lived in Los Angeles, say, then that may be a market worth specifically targeting. However I prefer an approach of letting the market speak to us through our results rather than trying to game it ahead of time. With that in mind a better approach is to advertise broadly and then look at your results to see if any location information shows up that would make targeted campaigns justified.

Cities	Selected Audience	Compare
Birmingham, Alabama, United States	0.2%	+100%
Huntsville, Alabama, United States	0.2%	+100%
Gilbert, Arizona, United States	0.2%	+100%
Pulaski, Arkansas, United States	0.2%	+100%
Boise, Idaho, United States	0.2%	+100%
Fort Wayne, Indiana, United States	0.2%	+100%
Lexington, Kentucky, United States	0.2%	+100%
Baton Rouge, Louisiana, United States	0.2%	+100%
Grand Rapids, Michigan, United States	0.2%	+100%
Springfield, Missouri, United States	0.2%	+100%

Birmingham, Alabama, United States
0.2% of selected audience
0.1% of Facebook users
Click chart to target

Well we've managed to come up with quite an audience that will bring a lot of fruitful results if you happen to sell a product that helps people deal with their debt problems. And if it also can be packaged with a Christian angle you've hit a gold mine. The thing is we are barely scratching the surface with the information presented here.

Let's return to the main tab and look back to the sidebar on the left side. First, lets look at Pages. You can click on the *Connected To* list to target people connected to one of your Facebook pages. This is useful if you want to market to people who have only already landed on your page and liked it etc. but not to others. Maybe these prospects are more primed for a sale.

On the other hand, you can also filter out people already connected to your page. Looking just below we see the *Not Connected* box. Use this and you can block people from the audience who've already been connected to your Facebook page. If you are just starting out, however, this isn't really worth bothering with.

Below this we find the Advanced tab. This is where a lot of interesting demographic details can be used to filter our audience. First, we can look at Language. If you're marketing in Canada, you might want to specify that the audience is English (or French) speaking. If you're marketing to Florida or the southwestern United States, you might want to specifically target people who's primary language is Spanish.

Next, we have Relationship Status. Since I've already specified in Demographics that I wanted married people, this has been selected for me here:

As you can see Facebook allows you to drill down in quite a bit of detail. Many marketers will be targeting Newlyweds or people who are Engaged.

Below this you can target Education level. In our case, we can expand our audience a little by selecting High School graduates. The audience increased in size to 2 M (an increase of about 500,000 – remember these are high school graduates pre-selected to like financial guru Dave Ramsey).

Looking down a little further, we see an input box we can use to target Job Title. But to the right graphs of occupation are provided for us. This is a great marketing tool right here – imagine being able to target people in our target demographic who work in sales. To do that simply click on the sales bar:

Scrolling down further on the left, we see *Market Segments*. This allows us to select so-called "Multicultural Identities" such as Asian Americans.

Below this, we have *Parents*. Clicking it open you see that there are many options allowing you to select parents with children up to 26 years old. Presumably, this allows you to market to parents that have or might have children living with them in the home.

Below that we see "Politics". This is not by party registration but instead allows you to select by self-reported "leaning" such as "very liberal", "moderate", or "conservative".

Finally, at the very bottom, we have Life Events.

Now scroll back up to the top. Going back to interests, this is a tool you'll use to refine most of your audiences.

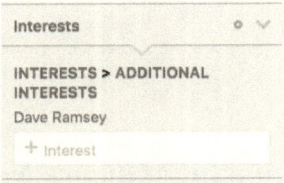

What if we want Dave Ramsey fans who are contemplating buying a home? We could type in Buying into the Interest box and see what comes up. Lo and behold we see:

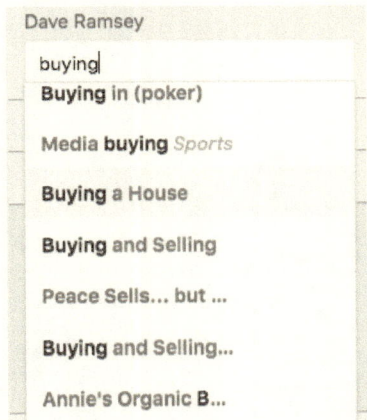

The interest drop down list is far from perfect – but it is a very powerful tool we can use in order to create our laser targeted audiences.

All this targeting isn't useful if we can't save our audience and use it later. Simply scroll to the top of the page and click Save from the list of buttons at the top. This opens a dialog window:

| Audience Name: | ve Ramsey Fans Married | Your audience will be available in the Audiences section of Ads Manager. |

Name	Size (People)	Modified	Owner	Preview
Double Down Casino	10m - 15m	2/23/17	David McMahon	Hover over an audience to view details.
European Slots	1.5m - 2m	3/1/17	David McMahon	
Hispanic Married Women in Texas with Children	150K - 200K	1/17/19	David McMahon	
House of Fun Slots	700K - 800K	3/5/17	David McMahon	
Phoenix Married Couples	100K - 150K	1/17/19	David McMahon	
Slotomania Jackpot Party	3.5m - 4m	5/18/17	David McMahon	

At the top, type in a meaningful *Audience Name* that you'll remember later.

So how do we use the audience? Now go back to the *Ads Manager* and create a new ad. When you go to the Audience section of your ad, you can click on *Use a Saved Audience* to pick the Audience you just created.

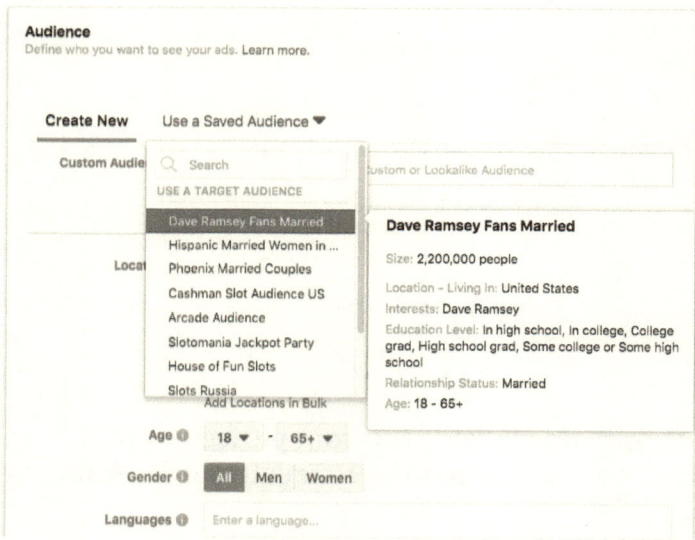

The audience has 2.2 million people but Facebook tells us that we'll reach up to 5,200 people per day – so we can advertise to this group a long time before running out of steam.

Action Point

You have two homework assignments for this chapter. First, using a product you already have or are planning to develop, use Audience Insights to create your first audience to target with advertising.

For your second assignment, just spend some time browsing various audience configurations and examine their page likes and occupations. Use this information to think of three new products you could create and sell to the audience.

Chapter 6: Lookalike Audiences

So far we've already seen the power of Facebook advertising just using ordinary targeting by interest, location, or demographics. Now we're going to explore a more advanced option that will increase the power of your advertising even more. It's called a *lookalike audience*.

In short a lookalike audience is an audience Facebook creates that resembles an audience you already have when it comes to key data points. For this to work you'll need to provide a source audience to Facebook in order for it to build this lookalike audience. Presumably the source is data gleaned from high value customer's who've bought your product or service. When creating a lookalike audience, Facebook will create a similar audience or group of people located in a country you select that have matching characteristics. This is done by picking a percentage of the country's population, ranging from 1% to 10%.

Create a lookalike audience to bring in even more customers and do it even easier than you did the first time around.

What is a lookalike audience? Basically, its new people that "look like" your customers. How do they look like them? They have similar characteristics that might make them more likely than not to buy your products:

- Same page likes
- Similar occupations
- Similar demographics
- Similar locations

As Facebook says:

When you create a lookalike from a Custom Audience that includes LTV, our system will find people similar to your highest value customers.

The idea is that by putting together this new audience of people who match in characteristics the people who've already bought from you, this will create an audience of new people that is predisposed to purchase or use your product or service.

For example, if you have a pre-existing internet business and you've been collecting email addresses, you can use this existing customer base as your source to have Facebook create a new group of people that are similar in key characteristics to those who've already signed on to your email list. If you're using MailChimp, you can import your list into Facebook.

Other options include using a Facebook Pixel to create an audience of people who've completed a defined conversion event on your website

We can also create lookalike audiences using people who've liked your page in Facebook or watch your videos. Let's have a more detailed look at these. First we'll take a look at video, since we've previously discussed running video ads.

I've run a lot of video ads. Something that would be useful for my marketing activities is to find a set of new people who match those in characteristics who've watched my videos for a given time period. For example I could specify that they watched at least 50% of the video.

To get started, the first thing we'll do is go to the Audiences dashboard. This can be found by selecting Audiences from the All Tools option in the drop down menu:

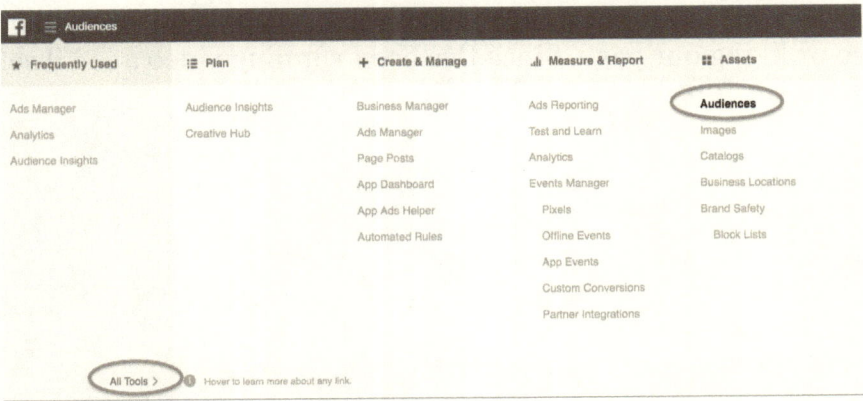

Looking at our list of audiences, in my case I see the following:

At the top, we'll click open the *Create Audience* drop down list and select Custom Audience.

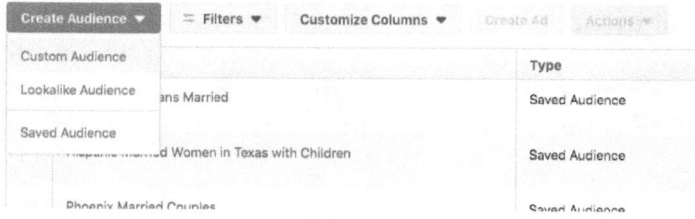

When you do this, you're given several options. The item of interest to us is *Engagement*. This allows us to select from people who've engaged with us on Facebook in some way, such as watching our video or liking our page. Since I've been running video ads I'll select Video at the top:

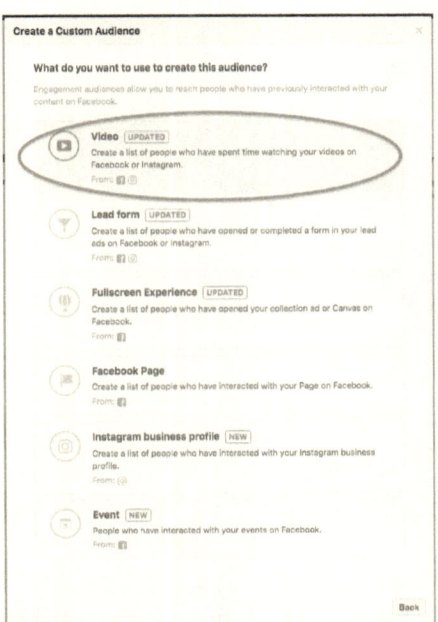

Next, you'll be asked to select criteria – as discussed above I'll pick people who've watched at least 50% of my video.

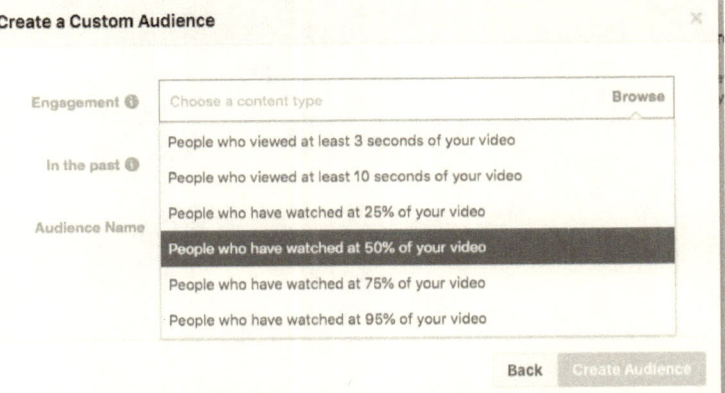

After you do this, you can select where they engaged with your video. For example, if it was on your Facebook page, you can select the page. If we want people from an advertising campaign we've used, we can do this by selecting Select by Campaign and then choosing the specific ad campaign. Here is what I get:

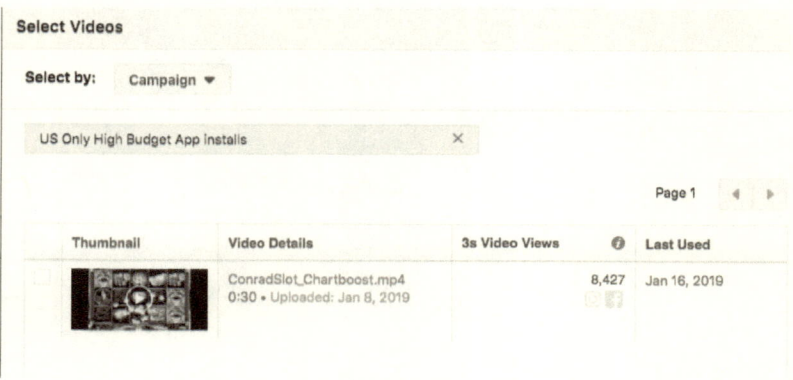

Then click confirm, and Facebook will go to work creating your audience. Depending on its size it can take it awhile to process the data. Facebook will then offer to create a new ad based on the audience you just created, or to create an expanded audience. The expanded audience is a lookalike audience – it will be a set of new people that match up in characteristics to people who've already watched my video 50% of the way through.

When you click Expand your Audience, you see a screen like this one:

First, select the country or region you want to target. In my case I will target the United States. Then you select the percentage of the people you want to include. It must be between 1% and 10%.

Notice that I've selected 5%. This creates quite a large lookalike audience for me – with 10.7 million people. Once I save it by clicking on *Create Audience*, it will be available for me to use in future marketing activities. Using the same methods we did before, we can create new advertisements and select Use Saved Audience, and we'll find it there.

This is very powerful stuff folks.

The data points that Facebook used to create the audience aren't available to us, but for the sake of creating a cartoon version of what's going on, let's suppose that all the people who watched my video to the 50% mark were blonde haired women aged 35-44 living in the southern US driving Chevy Impalas and named Jenny. What Facebook will do is create a new audience of women aged 35-44 living in the southern US driving Chevy Impalas named Jenny who haven't seen the video yet –but who are likely to respond in the same way because they are so similar. Again, I am making up the criteria to give you an overview of what's going on.

So what happens now is rather than show my ad to fairly random people (they like Slot Machine A), I've narrowed things down to people who watched Slot Machine A and who are extremely likely to watch 50% of the video –and download my app.

BOOM!

What do you think that does to conversion rates?

Our cost of acquisition will drop substantially.

Our conversion rates will increase substantially.

This seriously blows away other advertising methods that could be used. This is really laser targeted advertising. Undreamed of before.

When we went about creating our lookalike audience you may have noticed that there were many choices. You can choose based on people that liked your Facebook page and a set of other varied activities. In your case it might be picking people that have interacted with your brick and mortar store location or visited your website (you'll need Facebook Pixel for website traffic).

Let's take a quick look at another lookalike audience I could create – I will use App Activity. For App developers, this is powerful stuff.

Suppose that I created a new slot machine game. The bread and butter of these kinds of games are in-app purchases of coins. What if I could create a lookalike audience of people that are similar to those who have purchased coins inside one of my apps?

That's like creating an ATM machine.

The new lookalike audience would be composed of people who are prone to make in-app purchases in games. In practice, this means I can target people who are likely to make purchases and drive up the overall percentage of users downloading the game who are going to buy coins.

BOOM!

That means revenue will reach new heights!

Even if you don't have an app, we hope this example illustrates the power of using lookalike audiences. You can use a Facebook Pixel to build audiences based on your web traffic. For example maybe they've signed up for a news letter or taken other action on your site. This will create a primed audience ready to go you can advertise to who are prone to take similar actions.

Action Point

Now that you've gone through the steps of creating an ad and a Facebook page, and perhaps built up a customer list on your website, create a custom lookalike audience based on your results so far. Run a new ad campaign based on your lookalike audience and compare results.

Chapter 7: Creative Types

Now let's take a step back and think about the various creative types available with Facebook ads. The creative is the source material for the ad itself, such as a video. We've talked about this some already but lets look at the details of each.

Single Image

A single image ad should use a 1080 x 1080 pixel image, but you can use smaller images if you don't have one that size available. You can use stock images or upload your own images. You can use up to six images with your ad to actually create six different ads simultaneously. Another useful option is to use a different image for instagram, if you're using that placement. To use images on Instagram, they must be at least 500 x 262 pixels.

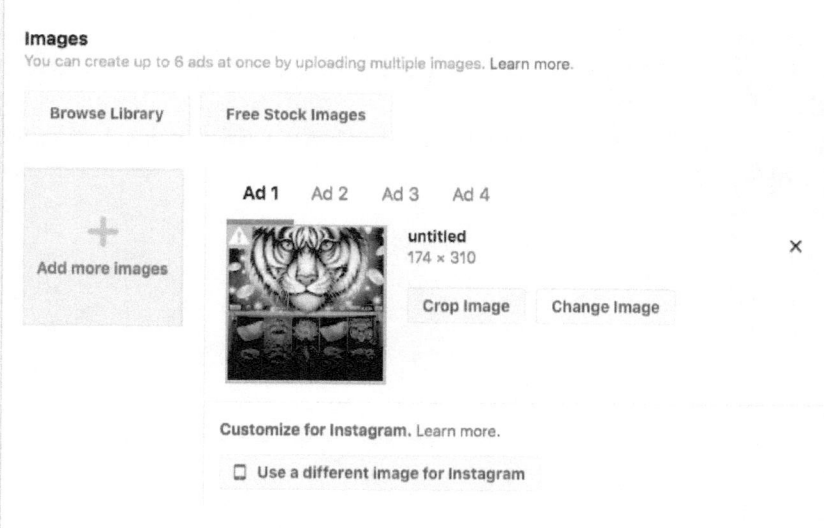

Facebook allows you to do split testing when creating single image ads using multiple images. A split test can run from 1-30 days and be used to determine which image produces the best results for your campaign.

The bottom line for the single image ad is it's the low budget option. Video is more engaging, but you might not have the resources to make a video ad.

Video Creation Kit

Just above "Images" you'll see a box describing the latest Facebook innovation, the video creation kit. If you're stuck in a situation of having to use still images to create your ads, you might want to have a look at the video creation kit because the bottom line is that video ads convert better.

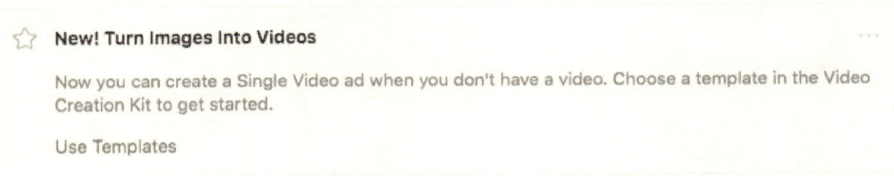

You can select either a square or vertical template. Square is nice since it fits right in the Facebook news feed.

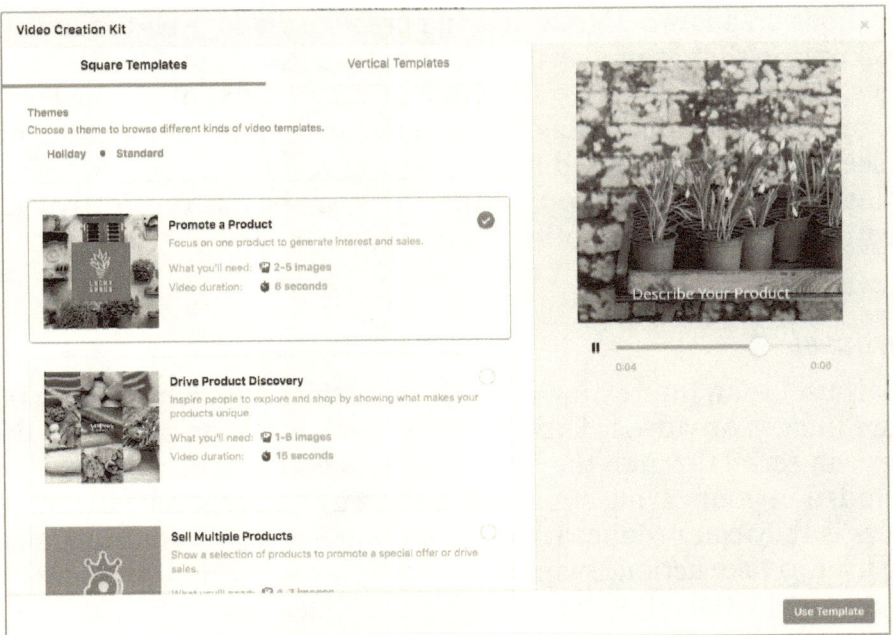

Each template option tells you how long the "video" it creates will be and how many images you need. The video will scroll through a series of images and logos that you add. You can preview the video on the right side, and you can add effects such as stickers, frames, and colors. For example, in my case I can create an add using still screenshots from my app in different scenes.

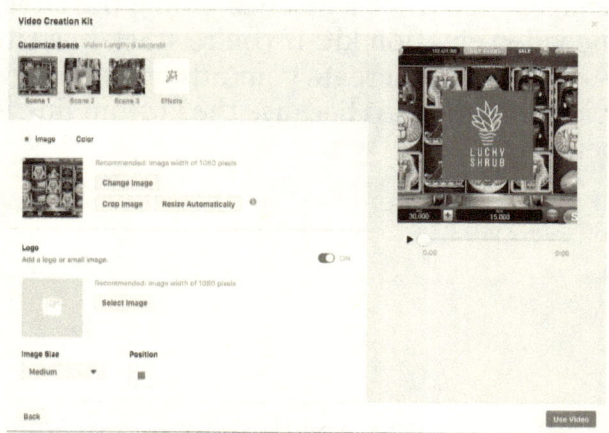

Slideshow

For those on a low budget who can't create a video, a slide show is a good option that is an alternative to a video kit. To make a slide show, you'll need at least 3 images and a maximum of 10 images. To use on Facebook and Instagram a slideshow can be a maximum of 15 seconds. Images should have an aspect ratio of 16 x 9 and the slideshow will run in a loop. A slideshow can be a very effective ad creative and is a better option than a single image.

Carousel

A carousel is an interesting upgrade to a slideshow, which has 2 or more images or videos. This is a more interactive format where the user can scroll through the individual images or videos you've included in your carousel. I haven't tried using carousel ads but my guess is they can produce high conversion rates because they call on the user to take action, swiping through the individual creatives used to make the ad. You can even put a slideshow into a carousel ad. Since you can put single images, videos, and slideshows as individual elements or "cards" in a single carousel ad, you might think of it as a "super ad".

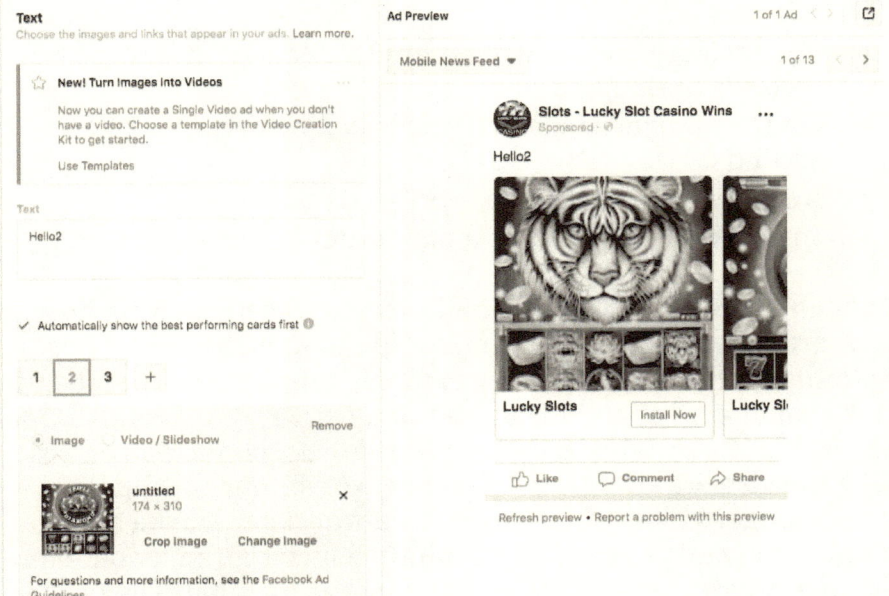

Instant Experience

Instant experience ads are for use on mobile devices. Since so many people are engaging with Facebook using their mobile devices, you can't go wrong with targeting them with your ads. If someone interacts with an instant experience ad it takes up the full screen. As Facebook puts it, it creates an "immersive experience". Formats that can be used with an instant experience ad include video, single image, carousel, slide show and collection. It also allows the use of fillable forms and multiple Instant Experiences can actually be linked together. This is a newer and more advanced ad format I've not experimented with.

Video

Since humans are visual creatures, video remains king. Video ads convert well – probably far better than any single image ad you can create - assuming you've made a reasonable video to use in your ad. Length of videos allowed depend on placement:

- On Facebook, a video can be up to 240 minutes long.

- On the Instagram feed, they can be 120 seconds or two minutes long.
- For Instagram stories maximum video length is up to 60 seconds or one minute.
- On the audience network videos can be between 5-120 seconds.
- Rewarded videos can be 3-60 seconds.
- In-stream videos can be a maximum of 15 seconds.

Although a 240 minute video is allowed on Facebook, that doesn't necessarily mean you should make a full length movie and post it. I've found that in an advertising campaign designed to get the user to take some kind of action, a video of length 15-30 seconds is ideal. Longer than that in the fast paced world of social media you risk losing the viewers attention. Of course we can imagine applications where a longer video might be more appropriate. Maybe a real estate agent wants to upload a 2 minute video tour of a home for sale. In any case, try and make it as short as possible. The trick is posting enough information to convey your message while still holding their attention.

An important point of data – Facebook allows a maximum video size of 4 GB and videos must be in mp4 or mov format.

Action Point

Create ads using each of the different formats but with everything else the same, and do split tests to see which works best for advertising your product or service. Allow the ads to run at least 3 days.

Chapter 8: ROI - Facebook Goals and Marketing Strategies

The number one rule when using Facebook Ads in your marketing plan is test, test, and test again. Always let the market speak to you about what works and what doesn't, including the painful reality that in some cases your product or service may not be desired at a profitable price point and cost per acquisition that can be reached in any realistic scenario. In that case its time to roll up your sleeves and come up with new ideas, incorporating what you've learned from your experience.

Now lets think about the basic advertising types offered by Facebook. For example, we've seen Reach, Brand Awareness, Lead Generation, and App Installs. You might think of one or more of these as "marketing" but really each are individual tactics that are part of your overall marketing plan.

Chances are, if you're reading this book you have a small business, potentially a one-man/one-woman or partnership. You're not Ford Motor Company or Mountain Dew.

Why do we mention this? Because the types of Facebook ads used will vary depending on the size of your company. The reality is that brand awareness is not something a small business should be pursuing. Let's look at it.

For brand awareness to work, you need to reach huge numbers of people. The basic idea behind brand awareness can be illustrated with a Chevy truck or Geico insurance commercial. Watching television you're going to be literally bombarded by ads for these products. You'll also be bombarded by ads for Taco Bell or Bud light.

Fact is most people don't give a damn but the goal of these advertising is brand awareness. So later on, a small fraction of people will get the itch to buy a new truck, and hopefully for GM the Chevy commercials that continuously air will place the idea of a Chevy truck at the forefront of their minds. So the first thing they might do is head to the nearest Chevy dealership or check it out online to get information on features and pricing.

In the event they buy a truck, they might be interested in checking out new insurance. Geico might come to their mind since its shoved down your throat ever 20 minutes you watch television (but you'll note the fierce competition, Liberty Mutual and Progressive advertise in huge amounts as well).

So what is the fundamental behind brand awareness? Its massive volume. Its volume so massive that no small business can possibly reach it. Think about it. Can you afford the budgets necessary to reach tens of thousands of Facebook users per day? Probably not. If you did you wouldn't be looking for advice on how to start running Facebook campaigns, you'd have a dedicated marketing department.

For that reason its my view that brand awareness campaigns on Facebook have limited value. A small business should be focusing on more direct action – acquire customer, get sale, repeat.

This brings to mind another option for Facebook ads – Reach campaigns. A Reach campaign is really just more Brand Awareness. It might be something in your toolbox but its not really recommended for small businesses in my opinion except as an adjunct tactic.

Page Likes

When advertising on Facebook the concept of a lookalike audience should always be foremost on your mind. Why? Lets think about a page like campaign.

When you're first starting out using Facebook to promote your product or service, you might consider advertising just to get page likes. Maybe you're a chiropractor and you've created a nice Facebook page describing some of the unique benefits your practice has to offer patients. You might have some engaging videos on y our page. So you run an ad campaign to get page likes and hopefully get some of your posts shared and commented on.

All well and good – now what?

Create custom audiences. You can create a custom audience of people who've liked the page, and then advertise to them more aggressively, for example getting them to sign up for your newsletter or offering a special deal to come in for a first time session. Create a lookalike audience to widen your base.

Retargeting

In any business using retargeting is a vital strategy. One of the most important groups of prospects you have are those who expressed interest in your product but didn't buy the first time around. Think of a furniture store. Someone is looking for a leather sofa and comes in and does some browsing. They might have seen one they like but aren't quite sure so leave without making a purchase.

What if you could show them an ad, with that brown leather sofa they liked now on sale for 25% off?

Facebook actually gives you all those customers. A furniture store can't specifically target them if they haven't given their phone number to a salesman, but we can go back and advertise to people who've seen our ads.

Filter out those who've purchased already and segment the into a different group that can be used to sell new related products to or for upsells. Custom audiences can be made of others, for example maybe someone who went to the shopping cart but failed to complete the purchase.

You might want to entice them by periodically reminding them of what they are missing by not purchasing. Its good to retarget regularly but to do so with fresh content. You can create videos and images to use in ads specifically designed to target these potential customers.

Traffic Generation

For internet marketers – which these days should include all business types – the ever present problem is traffic. Google Adwords seems to have lost its luster for me – too expensive. Also I like the focus on the buyer you get with Facebook, rather than on a particular search. So its useful to use Facebook advertising to push traffic to your site.

Lead Generation

Lead generation has some amazing features on Facebook but with some caveats. The best thing about using Facebook ads for lead generation is that it can greatly simplify the signup process. On mobile users interacting with Lead Generation ads get a prefilled signup form they can use. This is a great feature, since research shows the more hoops a customer has to go through the less likely they are to complete a purchase. Remove a step and you've upped the odds.

Unfortunately research also shows that the fact a customer has to put in some effort to sign up it filters out lurkers or people with only casual interest. The danger of the filled out Facebook form is that casual users will go ahead and sign up without any real inclination to make purchases. You don't just want leads, you want quality leads.

As always, the answer to this dilemma is testing. You can do split testing by having the sign up on your website and using a traffic campaign to direct users there, and then having a campaign using Facebook Lead Generation and see which method produces the best results.

Budgeting

Budget constraints are a huge issue. Its balance we seek. Penny pinchers never get anywhere but neither do people who fall into debt problems. With Facebook ads we want to avoid runaway spending.

The good thing about Facebook is the easy way you can turn campaigns on and off. Monitor your campaigns closely and when one appears to be getting out of control, just shut it off for a day, then look at your data and re-evaluate.

Alternatively, suppose we are talking about campaigns that are working very well. We will want to scale them up. However remember that Facebook campaigns have a bit of dynamic nature to them. The system is always learning, trying to get you the best results that it can given the constraints put in by you in the ad settings. Daily budget is one of those constraints. Changing the daily budget changes the conditions under which the campaign is operating.

Therefore we want to raise our budgets slowly. Let the campaigns learn – but don't risk throwing out what they've already optimized. A good rule of thumb is to raise at 10% per day except when budgets are really small.

If you are just starting, suppose your budget is $5 per day. You don't need to stick to the 10% rule in this case. You could raise first to $10 a day. Or alternatively, take 2 days, going to $7.50 on day 1 and then the second day go to $10. But don't jump to $40 or $100.

However if you're already at say $80 per day, then use the 10% rule and raise your budget to $88.

Although you can raise budgets daily, I like to stick to a three day rule to see how things work out. Remember in our discussions about creating new campaigns – I suggested letting campaigns run for three days. This gives them a chance to optimize and lets you see the real results they can produce.

The same principle is at work here. So when raising your budget, raise to your goal then wait at least three days before making another change. If raising the budget gets you to your desired goals for volume and cost per result, you might want to stop there and instead of raising the budget again to further increase volume, copy/clone the campaign.

Another tip to keep in mind is avoid making multiple changes at once. Suppose we have a campaign advertising in Irvine, CA with a daily budget of $40. If we get up in the morning and change locations to Irvine, Huntington Beach, Anaheim, and Newport Beach, and raise the budget to $60, but then find our cost per result increases, how do we know what the real factor was in causing the change in our cost?

So if you decide on a budget increase – do that slowly and by itself without making other changes.

If you're planning on expanding your campaign reach by adding locations or more demographics, either wait until the budget has settled (three day rule) or consider cloning the campaign instead. In fact in many cases cloning the campaign might be more desirable. In my case, advertising slot games nationwide, I've generally found its best to start with a campaign targeting the United States, and once its optimized rather than adding say Australia to the same campaign, I clone it. Then I edit the copied campaign to change the location from United States to Australia.

The advantage of this is I can isolate differences that might arise from advertising to people in a different location. In my case, maybe there are gender differences as opposed to the United States, or I might need to change the interests I've selected for Detailed Targeting.

Metrics for Success

There are many metrics for success. They could include page likes, shares, or comments on your postings. In the end however, its closing a sale that matters. Page likes are easy and done with a single mouse click. A lot of people will do a page like with zero intention of buying a product.

So you'll need to always focus on the end game – how many people bought and how much did it cost. In my case its easy – app installs and Facebook actually has that built in. Look into building your product sales directly to Facebook.

Always check rates of involvement for posts. Are people opening your video, but leaving it very early without producing a result? Are people leaving negative reactions or bad comments?

Be ready to abandon ad creatives that aren't working. If a video isn't producing sales, keep the ad the same and change the video.

Always clone/copy ads. There may be another reason the ad isn't producing – you might have the wrong interests in your detailed targeting or have bad locations or demographic choices. There is only one way to check that – keep the old video and make changes to those selections.

But always be on the lookout for content that generates negative reactions. If people are leaving negative reactions to your video then you need to swipe out the video. Another thing to consider is changing the type of ad. Maybe in your case video isn't the best option and its better to use a slideshow.

Facebook Pages

A Facebook page for your product or service isn't just necessary for some types of Facebook ads, it's a useful tool but you shouldn't inflate its importance.

I say this with the idea of blogging in mind. The reality is, unless you're a celebrity a Twitter feed or blogging is likely going to be a complete waste of time. Do you want to spend 8 hours a day writing articles and tweeting, to get 50,000 followers a year from now? Its probably not the best use of your time.

A Facebook page has a lot of benefits.

- Brand awareness
- Easy customer engagement
- A place where customers can leave feedback
- A place where you can directly address problems

With that in mind, its good to keep the page active. Post on it around 2 or 3 times a week. Seeing posts on it will get customers interested. You can post new videos and offer special deals. Do it even if right now your page isn't getting any views.

When a prospect does land on your page and it seems more active, its going to generate more interest. They might comment on a video or like a post. If customers make comments or leave feedback, *always* engage with the customer. Be sure to thank them for commenting.

This is true especially when an irate customer leaves negative feedback.

Maybe 95% of your customers have a positive view, so you might feel like you can ignore the unhinged crazy poster that leaves harsh criticism and makes nasty remarks.

That's not a good strategy. Always engage and always thank them even if they've told you to jump off a cliff in completely rude fashion.

If they list specific things they don't like – thank them and tell them your research team is looking into addressing the issues for your next product update. Publicly offer them a refund or discount or some other perk.

This way you communicate to the lurking customers who may be happy now that you're always willing to satisfy the customer. This will make them more confident in making future purchases from you.

When maintaining your Facebook page, don't always make it about the hard sell. You can use some posts to highlight sales, product features, and other deals – but you'll want to incorporate some other relevant content as well. Customers appreciate someone who is genuinely interested and not just looking to "make a buck".

So if you're selling a dog training course, don't always post links to your sales page. Spend some time posting related content without any reference to your product or making a sale. The goal here is to drive customer engagement and start creating the idea of a community.

If you're selling Air Fryers, don't always post a purchase link – spend time posting some recipes for Air Fryers.

Facebook Group

This brings us to the idea of a higher end option you have to drive engagement beyond just a Facebook page. You can create a Facebook Group as well. This can be made exclusive, so a group could require an invite to join and you can restrict it to people who've purchased one of your products.

A Facebook Group provides many features and benefits:

- Creates a feeling of exclusivity if the group is closed, enhancing the idea of community.
- It facilitates discussions between your customers.
- It gives you a place to converse only with people who have already bought one of your products.
- It provides a place for genuine sharing of information.
- A Facebook Group is a place where you can upsell existing customers.
- A Facebook Group is a place where you can beta test new products and get feedback before selling to the general public.
- Give members of the group some freebies to enhance customer loyalty.
- Offer them early bird specials.
- Offer premium customer service (maybe for an extra fee)
- Follow group discussions among members to brainstorm new related products that solve their needs.

ROI

Remember that our goal is to acquire a customer at the lowest possible cost, and create LTV. If your ROI is not where you want it to be then look at places along the chain where you can implement refinements in your marketing plans. This can include creating custom/lookalike audiences, refining ad spend, lowering cost of acquisition, increasing customer engagement, or trying different advertising strategies.

Action Point

After you've built a customer base of 50 people who've bought your product or service, create a closed Facebook group and invite them to join. Offer them an enticement like 3 months of customer service or a free report.

Chapter 9: Boosted and Promoted Posts

There was a time that "guerilla marketing" was all the rage. Think of it as using free, but unusual and clever marketing techniques to create awareness of your business.

But like blogs and even SEO the benefits for *most of us* are dubious. Sure, some people are going to use SEO and get on page one of Google. But anyone with any sense is using SEO, has that occurred to you? So how are you going to get ahead of them?

In my view –again such techniques will work for some, just like over time some will get a blog following – for most small businesses the best option is pay for traffic. Yes, even after all the tech wizardry and supposed "freemium" lifestyle its back to basics.

However there are some exceptions you can use in conjunction with your paid Facebook advertising that can be helpful to drive customer engagement and even turn them into paying customers. One of these techniques is the supposed "boosted post".

Using a Boosted Post is a two step operation in the simplest case. Let's look at it.

First, go to your menu under the Facebook Ads Manager dashboard, and select All Tools→Page Posts.

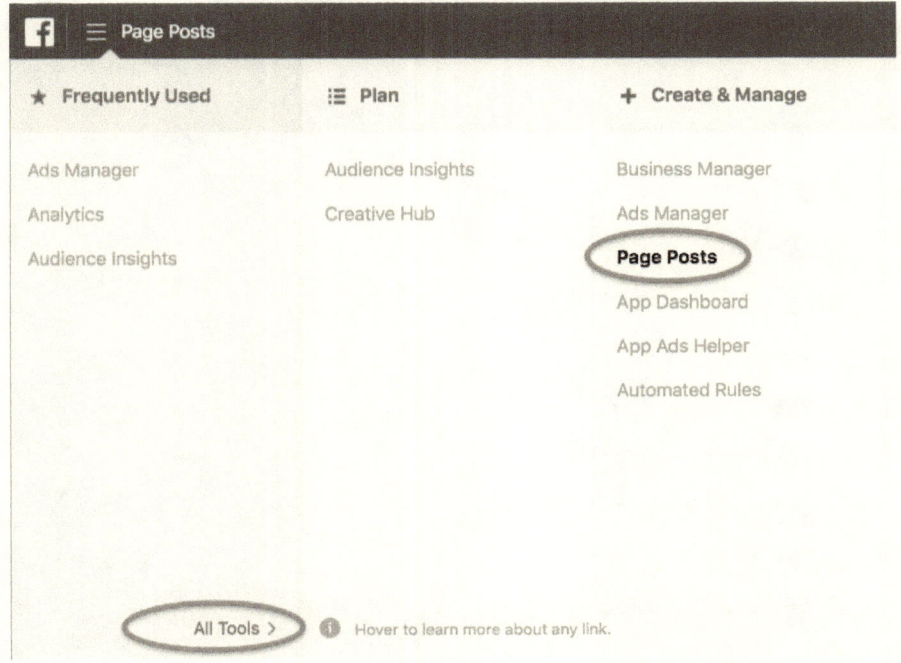

This will bring up your posts in a list format.

You can either create a new post or click on one from the list you want to promote. This will open it in a window with the option to Boost the Post. I've selected a video ad that I've previously posted:

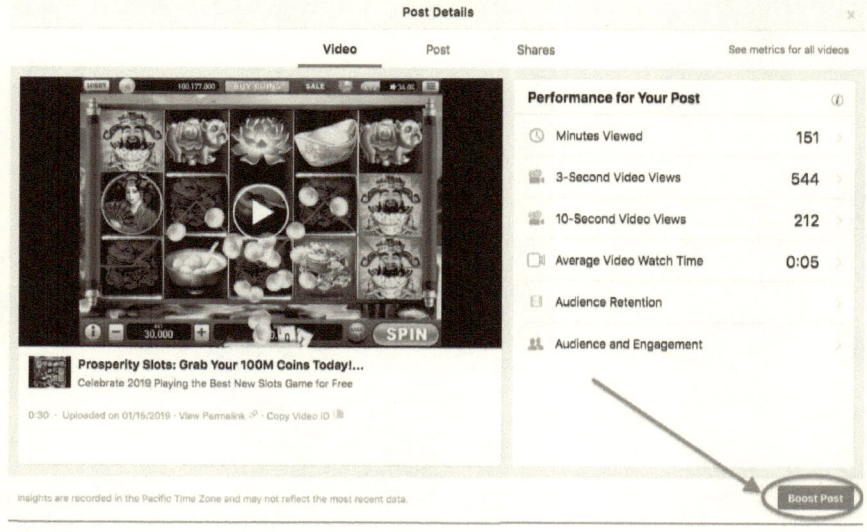

Here, you have an option to Boost the post by selecting people you choose with targeting. Keep in mind that you're essentially creating an ad and will have to set a daily budget and so on.

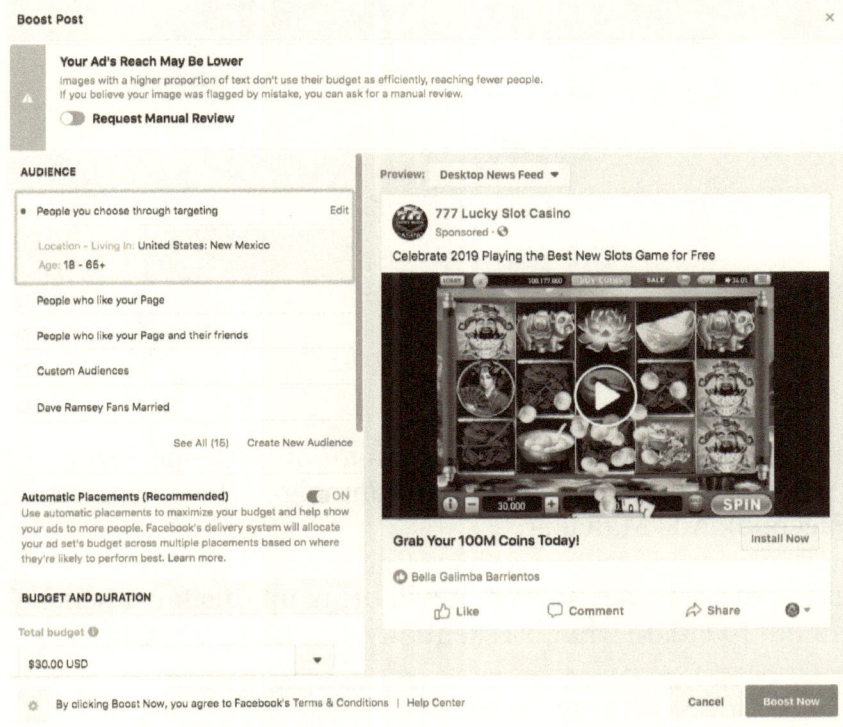

In my case, it's a little easier since I'm trying to drive installs of my mobile app. So I can direct users from the post right to the App Store and get downloads. In your case, you might have a website where you want traffic. Make sure you have Facebook Pixel setup for that first. If you are trying to promote a mobile app – you'll need to install the Facebook SDK prior to launching. In either case, you can edit the *People you choose through targeting* option to refine the audience who will see the post.

When you scroll down the left side of the popup window, you'll see options for budget and how long you will run the campaign and if you're sending people to a website an option for Facebook Pixel.

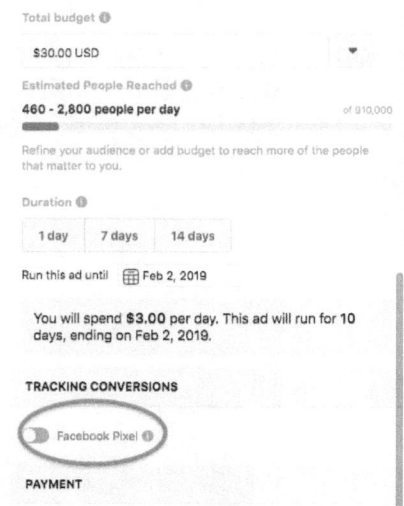

Once you've saved everything, you can monitor the performance of your post as you would a regular ad campaign. This is done from the Facebook Ads Manager.

If you opt to create a new post, it will bring up this form which you can fill out to create what is essentially another type of ad:

If you want to "promote" a post rather than boost an existing post, go to:

http://facebook.com/ads/create

and create a new ad, selecting *Engagement*.

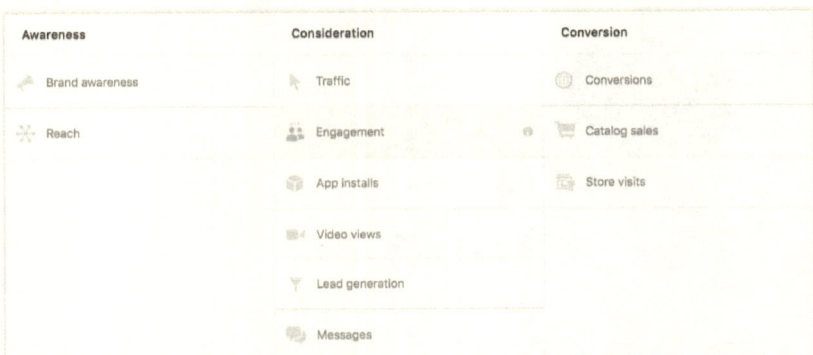

Engagement offers three options. Select the option you prefer.

From here on out, the procedure is like creating a standard advertisement. The suggested daily budget is $11, I'd advise starting out at $3 and working your way up gradually.

Boosting Posts from your Timeline

An easy way to boost posts is to do it from the timeline on your Facebook page. Simply find the post you want to promote, and click the *Boost Post* button:

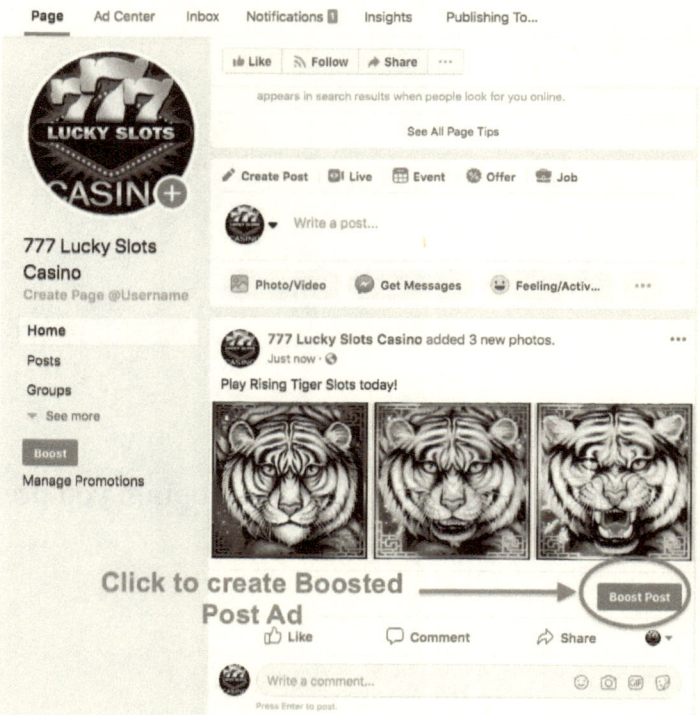

When you click the Boost Post button, you'll get the same popup windows we went through earlier when creating it from Ads Manager. It's a fast and easy way to turn a post into an ad.

Action Point

Assuming you're maintaining an active Facebook page for your business, find a popular post with some likes and engagement like comments. Click the Boost Post button and try a 3 day campaign. Set a low budget if its your first time testing this technique.

Chapter 10: Facebook Pixel

If you have your own website the mysterious *Facebook Pixel* is a useful tool you must use in conjunction with your advertising. And what exactly is this secret sounding device? Its simply a bit of code you incorporate into your website to track user activity on the site.

Your Facebook Pixel will have two basic parts:

- Base Code: Keeps track of all traffic to your site.
- Event Code: Event codes are used to track various events on your web pages.

There are many different events you can add to your Facebook Pixel for your website. Some of these include:

- Add to cart.
- Enter payment info.
- Search for product.
- Lead (after someone opts-in to your email newsletter).
- Purchase (from your thank you page after purchase completed).

As you can see, using the Facebook Pixel event codes can produce a complete picture of what is happening on your website.

If you are using third party tools for your website, many of them allow you to use Facebook Pixels. Please check with your provider for details.

Creating a pixel is done from the Ads manager. Open your menu and select All Tools, then look under *Measure & Report*. *Pixels* is under *Events Manager*.

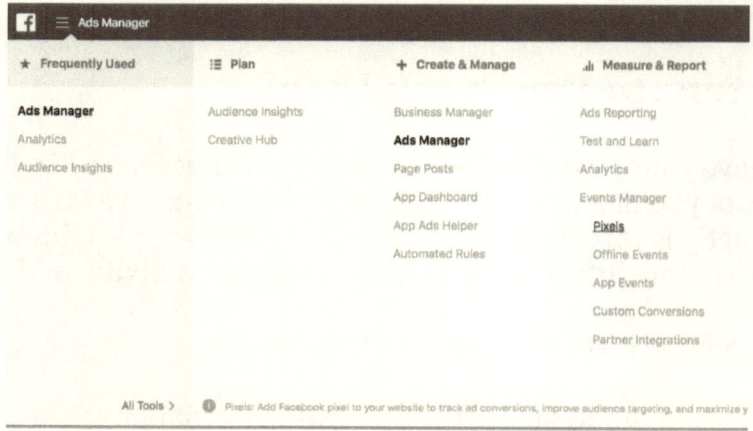

Facebook lets you use "Tag Manager" for third party sites or you can install the pixel yourself.

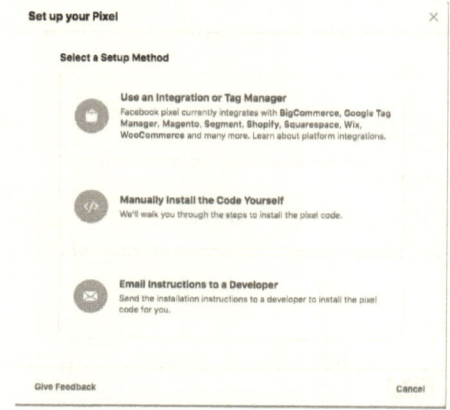

Alternatively, if you have hired a developer to manage your website, you can have Facebook email install instructions directly to the developer.

Why Use It

The reason you'll want a Facebook Pixel on your site is you can use it to create ads that target it. More to the point, you can advertise to people who've triggered certain events on your website. Earlier we discussed not forgetting customers that don't convert right away.

You can use a Facebook Pixel to target customers that went to your sales page but didn't purchase.

Alternatively, you could use it to target customers who viewed part of a video on your website but didn't finish it.

Another useful application is using it in conjunction with lead generation. If someone signs up for your email list, the Pixel will track all users who signed up and arrived to your thank you page. Then you can use the Pixel to run a targeted campaign just to those specific customers, who after getting their "Free Gift" in exchange for signing up for the email newsletter can be targeted to buy products.

Or lets say you're interested in running an ad campaign for an upsell. The Pixel can track people who've made a purchase and landed on the Thank You page for that action. You can advertise an upsell to that group.

And how much easier is this than the traditional web business setup of ten years ago? The Pixel does all the heavy lifting for you. You just get on the Facebook Ads Manager page and create ads targeting what you want.

Data collected by the Pixel can be viewed on the Pixel page from your Ads Manager.

Chapter 11: Common Mistakes

It's pretty easy to create Facebook ads. Its also easy to make mistakes. Let's go over some of the pitfalls you want to avoid.

Setting Initial Budgets to High

The first mistake you really want to avoid – in particular to avoid driving yourself in to bankruptcy by spending unnecessary advertising dollars – is setting your initial budget too high. By too high I actually mean the recommended Daily Budget that Facebook gives you. It can't be said enough, start with bottom level bids and slowly work up. If Facebook recommends $40 in ad spend, don't take that recommendation. Start at $5 or $10.

Not Letting Ads Run Long Enough

You run your campaign the first day. In todays world of instant gratification, you find yourself completely frustrated. The ads been running for six hours and you've only gotten two downloads of your app or two likes of your post. You shut the ad off and create a new one with different settings. Well, that's a bad move. The rule I apply in all things Facebook is the three day rule. Give every ad or every change you make three full days to run and play out. Think of Facebook ads as an artificially intelligent system that needs to learn. You have to give it enough time to optimize. If after three days you're still not seeing results, then look at your data to see why and only then make the changes.

Not Having Enough Ads

Remember the market always speaks. To let it speak to you, you have to ask it enough questions. One common failure is people create one Facebook ad and then aren't happy with the results. You should be creating as many as possible that will fit in your budget. We spent an entire chapter discussing it but it bears repeating. The more ads you put up the more data you collect and the more reach and lower costs of acquisition you'll see in the long term. If you're looking for a daily budget of $50, but can afford to go with $100 for 3 days or so, then go for $100 of total ad spend but create 20 ads with $5 as the daily budget setting for each. Every three days shut off the ads that aren't working and refine down to the ads you want to keep in your campaign. If you have one ad and your competitor is running 10 – you're losing the battle for customers.

Not Using Lookalike Audiences

Technology gives people a lot of headaches, and a lookalike audience is a bit of a hassle. But there is no more powerful tool. After you've collected data by starting with a general audience, create lookalikes to get stellar conversion rates and drive down those costs of acquisition.

Not Doing Research

Make sure you take time to play around with Audience Insights. Find out what pages they are liking. Find out where they live and what their occupations are. Check interests and see how that changes page likes. Design new ads that will target people based on their page likes. This research tool is a huge advantage you need to use in your marketing.

Lack of a Strategy

Simply throwing up Facebook ads is a tactic. And it will probably work, since Facebook is such an effective marketing platform. But doing that without an overall strategy is a recipe for failure. Before you start advertising set down in the clearest terms possible what your goals are. Go through each of the Facebook ad types and select that ones that best help you reach your goals. Plan your budgets accordingly by having a clear idea of how many customers you want to acquire on a daily basis.

Lack of a Schedule and not Maintaining Pages

Scheduling is important for running ads and managing your Facebook Page. For running ads, know when your customers are the most interested in taking the time to respond to your ads. To find out you have to run ads 24/7 to determine days of the week and time of day. Second, make sure you're keeping your Facebook page engaging. Don't make it look like a dead page. Some people seeing your ads are going to check it out. To put your best foot forward post on a scheduled basis, even if its just twice a week.

Being Afraid of Killing What Doesn't Work

If your ad set is failing to deliver customers, page likes or whatever at a price that you are aiming for then kill them off. Again, stick to the three day rule and give everything at least three days to optimize.

Set a Cost Target

Know what your cost target is. For me its 85 cents to acquire a new customer. If your ads aren't approaching the cost target, they need to be turned off.

Keep Up With the Times

The world of technology is in constant flux. You need to keep yourself familiar with Facebook. Know what's changing whether its their policies or whether they are introducing new tools or killing off old tools. Ad campaigns that work this year may not work next year. Its kind of irritating, we'd all like to set things running and spend the next five years playing golf. But we can't do that. Keep up and adapt are the rules. Failure to adapt to the ever present changes in the tech world means death for your business.

Pay Attention to Placements

We discussed this early on in the book. Placements are vital. What we're talking about here are Instagram vs. Facebook or Messenger and all the subcategories therein. Be sure to monitor all of them closely and shut off placements that don't work for you. Too many small businesses simply go with Automatic Placements and don't think about it after that. Don't be one of those people – you might be flushing money down the toilet without realizing it.

Failure to Switch Up Creatives

You made a great video for your ad. You run the ad and it converts great. Don't become too attached to it. Do you see Geico running the same commercials they did five years ago or even last year? Probably not. Their wildly successful cave man theme isn't used anymore. Your ads become stale over time, so be sure to regularly refresh the content you advertise.

Don't Go On the Fly

Its too easy to create Facebook ads. Don't just fire it up and create an ad. Do your research beforehand. I strongly recommend using Audience Insights. Assuming you've actually read this book, then you remember the chapter where we started off with married couples and then found out debt was a major concern, and then found out that Christian themed advisors were near the top of their interests.

You can use that information in a myriad of ways – not just when saving your audience. Take that information and use it to write a series of headlines and text to include in your ads – or to select ad creatives. Have your target groups ready along with customized creatives and headlines ready before even taking the first steps to actually create the ads.

Conclusion

Thanks for taking the time for reading this book and making it all the way to the end. We hope you have found the information practical and useful, and we wish you the best of success in your business endeavors.

www.ingramcontent.com/pod-product-compliance
Lightning Source LLC
Chambersburg PA
CBHW020553220526
45463CB00006B/2282